IMAGES OF ENGLAND

WINSON GREEN
AND BROOKFIELDS

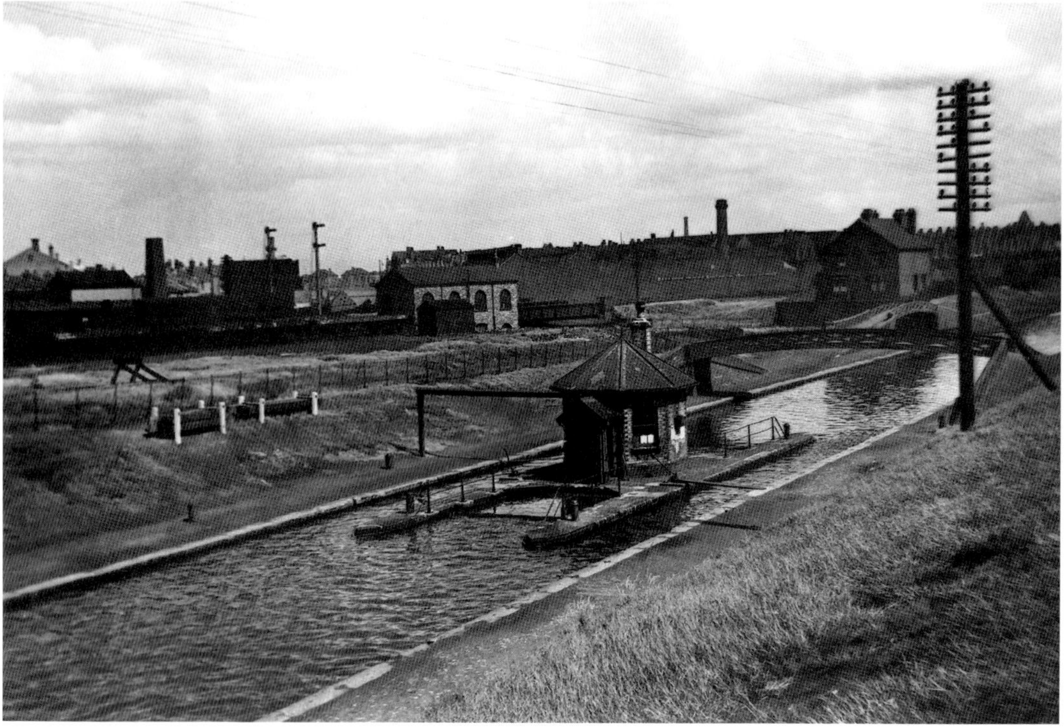

IMAGES OF ENGLAND

WINSON GREEN AND BROOKFIELDS

PETER DRAKE

TEMPUS

Frontispiece: Winson Green tollgate on the Birmingham-Wolverhampton Canal. The photograph, taken from the feeder, is by E.H. Sargeant. The straight lines of the Thomas Telford Canal, shown here, contrasted vividly with the earlier Brindley Canal which had followed the land's natural contours. The base of the tollgate still exists, as does the old canal house.

First published 2003

Tempus Publishing Limited
The Mill, Brimscombe Port,
Stroud, Gloucestershire, GL5 2QG

© Peter Drake (for Birmingham Libraries), 2003

The right of Peter Drake (for Birmingham Libraries) to be identified as the Author of this work has been asserted in accordance with the Copyrights, Designs and Patents Act 1988.

All rights reserved. No part of this book may be reprinted or reproduced or utilised in any form or by any electronic, mechanical or other means, now known or hereafter invented, including photocopying and recording, or in any information storage or retrieval system, without the permission in writing from the Publishers.

British Library Cataloguing in Publication Data.
A catalogue record for this book is available from the British Library.

ISBN 0 7524 3049 1

Typesetting and origination by Tempus Publishing Limited
Printed in Great Britain by Midway Colour Print, Wiltshire

Contents

	Introduction	6
one	Early Days	9
two	The Institutions	23
three	Pubs	35
four	Churches and Schools	55
five	Shopping on the Dudley Road and the Flat	75
six	The Workplace	87
seven	Leisure Activities	99
eight	Buses and Trams	107
nine	Street Scenes	117
	Acknowledgements	128

Introduction

Probably the best description of the size of the district covered by this book comes from a contributor to the excellent website devoted to recalling Winson Green and Brookfields. He writes:
> Looking back you do not realise how small our bit of the world we lived in was. I reckon that if you put a circle within a half-mile radius of where you lived most people would have lived at least ninety percent of their lives in that circle.

Simply described, the district lies in the area between Birmingham and Smethwick, touching the Edgbaston boundary on one side and Handsworth on the other. The demarcation with Smethwick was a clear-cut one according to those who lived on the Birmingham side. As one Birmingham correspondent to the website put it:
> We were citizens of a major modern city – they were the inhabitants of a small, grimy, industrial town, all but left behind in the Industrial Revolution. We worked in modern factories conducting precision engineering. They slaved in smoky old foundries making rough-arsed castings.

The history of Winson Green and Brookfields is unlike that of most of Birmingham's other inner city areas. The district was just far enough outside the town to be separate but it was never an established village. The earliest mention of Winson Green was in 1327 referring to a few herders' cottages somewhere near the site of the present Wellington and Bryant streets. A Dudley Road existed in medieval times as the route from Dudley Castle to Birmingham. In the eighteenth and early nineteenth centuries the town of Birmingham was divided into two parts; the built-up centre known as The Town, and the The Foreign just outside the centre. Winson Green and Brookfields, although very close to The Town, were very definitely The Foreign.

As far back as medieval times Birmingham Heath, the centre of Winson Green and Brookfields, was largely uninhabited heath land overgrown with gorse, ling and bracken. The Heath was dotted with the occasional settlement which was connected by pathways. The topography of the district showed that the land was fairly barren and lacked any real agricultural value. This situation continued right up to the end of the eighteenth century. Essentially up until then there was very little history to record. Apart from the isolated houses the Heath seemed to act as the premier recreation ground for the Town. The Heath provided exercise and parade grounds for the numerous military associations of 'Loyal Volunteers' soldiers who paraded there from the end of the eighteenth century. There is some evidence that on the Handsworth side of the Heath the area was home to such unsavoury activities as bullfights, bear-baiting and cock fighting. Prizefights took place in obscure parts of the Heath drawing vast crowds.

The first real development was the opening of the nearby Soho manufactory in the 1765. Matthew Boulton's new factory was the first change to the area's landscape since the medieval period. Boulton himself described the immediate vicinity of the factory which covered Hockley and Soho:
> I founded my manufactory on one of the most barren commons in England where there existed but a few miserable huts filled with idle, beggarly people who, by the help of the common land and a little thievery made shift to live without working.

The immediate consequence of this new manufactory with its thousand workers was that these workers needed to be housed fairly close to the factory. So Winson Green started to be built up. As a contemporary Directory noted 'The lord of the manor has exterminated these very poor cottages and hundreds of clean comfortable houses are found in their place.' The second consequence, although one delayed by many years, was the enclosure of the Heath. This happened at the turn of the nineteenth century, a late date for the enclosure of common land, no doubt due to the relative infertility of the land on the Heath. Enclosure was necessary to build the houses and roads for the new industrial developments following in the wake of the Soho manufactory. Workers houses needed to be built on legally ratified plots of land. Eight new roads were made initially, the main ones being Park, Lodge and Bacchus Roads and Heath Street. Winson Green Road was described as 'an ancient road leading to Winson Green'. Other landowners rented out portions of land for farming and grazing.

More industry came to the district on the back of canal building. The first Birmingham canal was built across the Heath in the 1760s, the canal bringing coal from Wednesbury to Birmingham in a much more economic way than by cart along the Dudley road. Although it had been turnpiked in 1760, the road did not have a macadam surface till the early years of the nineteenth century and a contemporary report in 1783 dubbed its state as 'despicable beyond description'. The canal was completed in 1772. Unfortunately its construction was not without tragedy. The *Aris's Gazette* reported on 24 July 1769:

> *Early on Saturday morning last a little beyond Winson Green in the Birmingham Canal Navigations, the Earth fell suddenly and killed John Lester, one of the workmen, occasioned it is thought by the heavy rains on Friday evening.*

Still by 1833 when the first Anglican church in the district, All Saints, was built, Winson Green and Brookfields was still predominantly rural in aspect. A writer looking back from the 1880s described an area fifty years before:

> *Farmhouses and cottages were scattered at intervals in the fields and lanes which surrounded the church on all sides. The church was the one prominent feature in the landscape, its dwarf spires rising above the surrounding trees. From Key Hill a rural lane led up to it, lined with hedgerows, amid which twined the honeysuckle and wild rose. Cornfields and hayfields were on either side of the road. A lane to the left led through meadows to Birmingham Heath. There was another way to the church from the bottom of Warstone Lane, over styles by pathways through the fields where murmuring brooklets crept along, where cowslips grew and ladysmocks all silvery white might be gathered for the trouble of stooping.*

Until the 1850s the appearance of Winson Green and Brookfields did not substantially alter, rather small isolated developments with houses in short terraces gradually appeared. Development was piecemeal as the pattern of land ownership was complex. Many of the new inhabitants to the area as shown in the 1851 census had moved in from outside Birmingham to work in a wide variety of trades, including the jewellery workshops in nearby Hockley.

Significantly for the future of Winson Green, the Birmingham Board of Guardians was one of the new landowners being awarded land between the Dudley Road and the meandering Birmingham-Worcester Canal. Birmingham Heath in the 1840s was still largely empty as the Town Council looked for sites for a new prison and a new workhouse. Within a few years, between 1848 and 1852, vast new institutions came to dominate the skyline in this part of Birmingham. The Borough prison was the first to be completed in 1848 providing unwanted accommodation for 340 prisoners. The prison's architect, Daniel Hill, then designed the nearby Lunatic Asylum. The Borough of Birmingham Workhouse, designed by J.J. Bateman, opened in 1852. A windmill on the Heath was demolished to make way for the new buildings; it is commemorated in the Old Windmill, the pub on the Dudley Road. It is interesting to see that when the Board of Guardians was assessing the site on the Heath for the workhouse a report stated that it was 'in some respect eligible, though rather too remote from the town' which shows how perceptions alter over the years. The workhouse was massive, intended to house up to 1,400 inmates and the buildings built continued to expand with a separate infirmary for the acutely ill opened in 1887.

Along with the new prison and workhouse the arrival of the Great Western trunk line in 1854 further developed the district. The railway connected Birmingham with Wolverhampton. 'The place became a wilderness of sand and brickwork, deep cuttings at one end and high embankments at the other completely altered the appearance of the spot'. The ensuing railway works and stations further transformed the area so that it began to lose its separate identity and become just another area of Birmingham. A second railway through the district, the London and North Western, opened in competition to the Great Western in 1886. The railways, the canals, the workhouse, infirmary and the prison also had one further consequence for the 'look' of Winson Green and Brookfields. It became and remains an area of walls – wherever you looked there seemed to be a long brick-built wall.

From the 1850s the infrastructure of the district began to develop; the schools, All Saints church school opened in 1844, Norton Street Board school in 1876, Dudley Road Elementary in 1878,

Foundry Road in 1883, Benson Road in 1888/9 and Handsworth New Road in 1901; the churches, All Saints by far the earliest in 1834, St Cuthbert's in1871, St Chrysostom's in 1885, St Patrick's Roman Catholic church in its present building in 1895, St Peter's off Spring Hill in 1900 and four years later Bishop Latimer; Spring Hill Library on 7 January 1893; the police station on the Dudley Road around 1880; the railway stations, Soho and Winson Green station in 1854 and Winson Green on the rival Stour Valley line in 1876; the recreation ground in Musgrave Road; nearly all the numerous pubs in the district, the corner shops and the large rows of shops on the Lodge and Dudley Roads.

The period also saw the loss of the few large houses that there had been in the district. Winson Green House and Winson House, the two substantial houses across from the prison, Bellefield with its landscaped grounds, Hockley Abbey and Summerfield House bought by the city to provide a park for Winson Green and Rotton Park all disappeared. Illustrations of most of these houses can be found in the first chapter, but sadly one of Bellefield does not seem to have survived.

From about 1910 no significant developments took place until the 1960s, principally because any new building would have meant the demolition of existing properties. There was simply no space. As a writer in 1880 put it: 'Passing through the district now it would scarcely be possible to find a vacant space large enough to gather one hundred people together on'. (This was to contrast with 1866 when a great Reform demonstration was held in Brookfields when over 100,000 were present). 'The district is one compact mass of buildings and about the only green spot is the All Saints churchyard, almost overtopped by the great Railway Works, and crowded out of sight by the surrounding houses.'

The majority of photographs in this book come from this time frame. It was a period remembered nostalgically by many former residents. There was little new building so the area remained settled, families helped each other out and a real sense of community was felt. There were however some real pockets of deprivation, as this newspaper report from the 1930s points out:

> St Cuthbert's sixty acres are not very pleasant. A railway and a canal run through. There are dirty back-to-back houses, gloomy courts and alleyways...the district suffers from a pathetic kind of poverty. There are a lot of cases of TB and MD and to me these tragic initials sound worse than the afflictions for which they stand – tuberculosis and mental deficiency. Most of the sickness, according to a local doctor, is due to semi-starvation. The vicar old me how fourty years ago Winson Green really was green, and carriages containing fine ladies and gentlemen used to roll up to the church. Since then factories and back-to-back dwellings have made the area congested and consequently poor.

Balanced against this was the community spirit engendered by the compactness of the area with the local shops and pubs and cinemas all within walking distance. Children went to local schools usually very close to their homes and made friends for life. The differing churches were central to the spiritual and social life of the community.

From the 1960s all this changed. Part of the impetus for this redevelopment came from war damage but most came from the desire of planners to improve the condition of housing in the area. Post-war a form of planning blight descended on the district. Rented houses were the norm with landlords not paying for repairs. Compulsory redevelopment followed and old families moved out, often to new flats and houses in the outer suburbs. The character of Winson Green and Brookfields changed. To quote a correspondent to the website 'very distinctive strangers predominantly uprooted and lonely men arrived in large numbers... the neighbourhood was wholly unprepared for different ways of living, strange aromas of spicy cooking'. Redevelopment in the district was not wholesale or comprehensive as it had been in other inner parts of the city, rather it was piecemeal and long drawn out creating the Winson Green and Brookfields which exists today. Undoubtedly too much was destroyed, too many corner shops and pubs, too many perfectly serviceable terraces but the planners had learnt from the mistakes of the early sixties and kept the tower blocks out.

Perhaps the most evocative images in the book are those of the Flat, the erstwhile shopping centre on the flat part of Lodge Road. Now with half of the shops demolished to make way for the Middleway and the few remaining ones looking pretty forlorn I hope the photographic memories preserved in this book will pay tribute to an area and a working class community which has always had to battle to survive.

one

Early Days

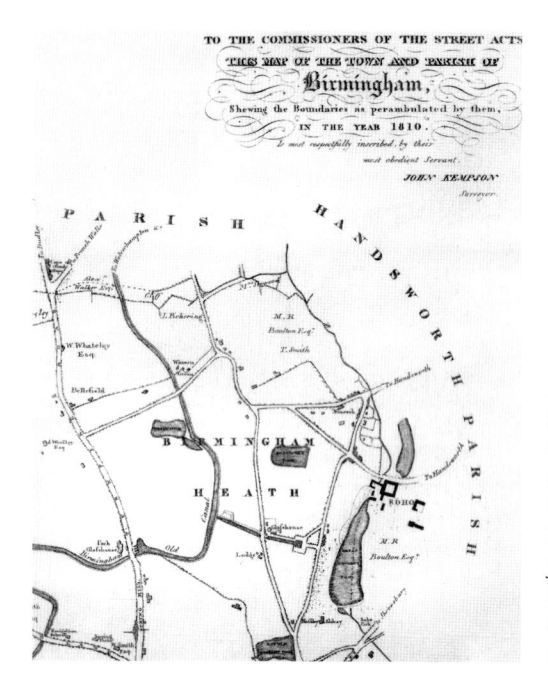

1810 Street Commissioners map 'showing the Boundaries of the Town as Perambulated by them'. Dudley Road, the Turnpike road, runs up the left-hand side from Spring Hill to the Smethwick boundary at the Cape. Two country houses, Summerfield House, the residence of J. Wooley, and Bellefield House flank the Dudley Road. The Street Commissioners were responsible for all the thoroughfares in the area except the turnpikes.

Winson Green House from a daguerreotype taken by a Miss Wilkinson in 1841. Apart from the caption stating that the photograph is in the Kensington Museum, this was all the information that was at hand about this intriguing image. However behind the photograph is an interesting story. Miss Wilkinson was Elizabeth Stockdale Wilkinson, a relative of the Boulton family and a frequent visitor to Soho House. Along with a Mr W.G. Alston, possibly of a firm of colour makers based in the town centre, Elizabeth Wilkinson experimented with the then very new science of photography. Mr Alston was then living at Winson Green House. This daguerreotype is almost certainly the earliest surviving image of anywhere in Birmingham.

Two further illustrations of Winson Green House taken around the time of Boulton's pamphlet and used to show that the original image was of the House. The story behind the photograph is partly told in the pamphlet written in 1865 by M.P.W. Boulton, a nephew of Elizabeth Wilkinson, entitled 'Remarks Concerning Certain Pictures Supposed to be Photographs of an Early Date.'

Above: The same house? This photograph was presented to the Library in 1905 by a lady who well remembered 'the old house with its very large grounds opposite the gaol. It is all built over now!' The house was probably built for James Turner, a local button manufacturer in the early nineteenth century. Two lodge houses associated with the main house survive on the Handsworth New Road next to Dolman's garage.

Left: Richard Tangye, the well known engineer, industrialist and travel writer who lived at Winson Green House in the 1870s. He was knighted in 1894, the year he left Birmingham for Cornwall. He played a large part in the religious, political and municipal life of Birmingham and Smethwick, and he was also a generous benefactor to the City Museum and Art Gallery.

These two views show Hockley Abbey. On the fringes of Soho and Winson Green, Hockley Abbey was another intriguing building. It was not an 'abbey' at all, nor despite its appearance was it older than the end of the eighteenth century, and was probably built in 1780. A local manufacturer, Richard Ford, built it as his own residence and deliberately designed it in a picturesque style as a bona fide ruin. It even bore the false date 1473. The exterior was covered with slag from the ancient iron works called Aston Furnace near the lower end of Summer Lane. It was consequently known as the Cinder House.

Above: An illustration of the Abbey, taken from Dent's *Old and New Birmingham*. The Abbey was demolished not long after this image was taken. A nineteenth century paper described it as 'a mean and ill contrived house and not to be compared to a £50 house of today'.

Right: George Frederick Muntz, the famous Birmingham political reformer and one of the founders of the Birmingham Political Union, who lived at Hockley Abbey in the 1830s. All trace of the Abbey has gone after its demolition in the 1860s. The land was used for housing, but at the junction of the new streets, Ford and Whitmore streets, John Rabone & Sons built their Hockley Abbey measuring tapes works. The Abbey is nowadays recalled in the name Abbey Street off the Lodge Road.

Summerfield House on the site of the present Summerfield Park in about 1820. Its history is unclear though it is probable that a Dr Hinckley who owned part of Rotton Park built it in the late seventeenth century. For many years it was the residence of Lucas Chance. It was taken over by the Corporation when the House and its gardens were bought for a much needed public park.

The old bandstand in Summerfield Park in 1892, with Mr Price on the left and Mr Keeley on the right. The park has always been one of the few green areas close to Winson Green, and a favourite spot for mothers to take their children away from the congested streets for fresh air and recreation.

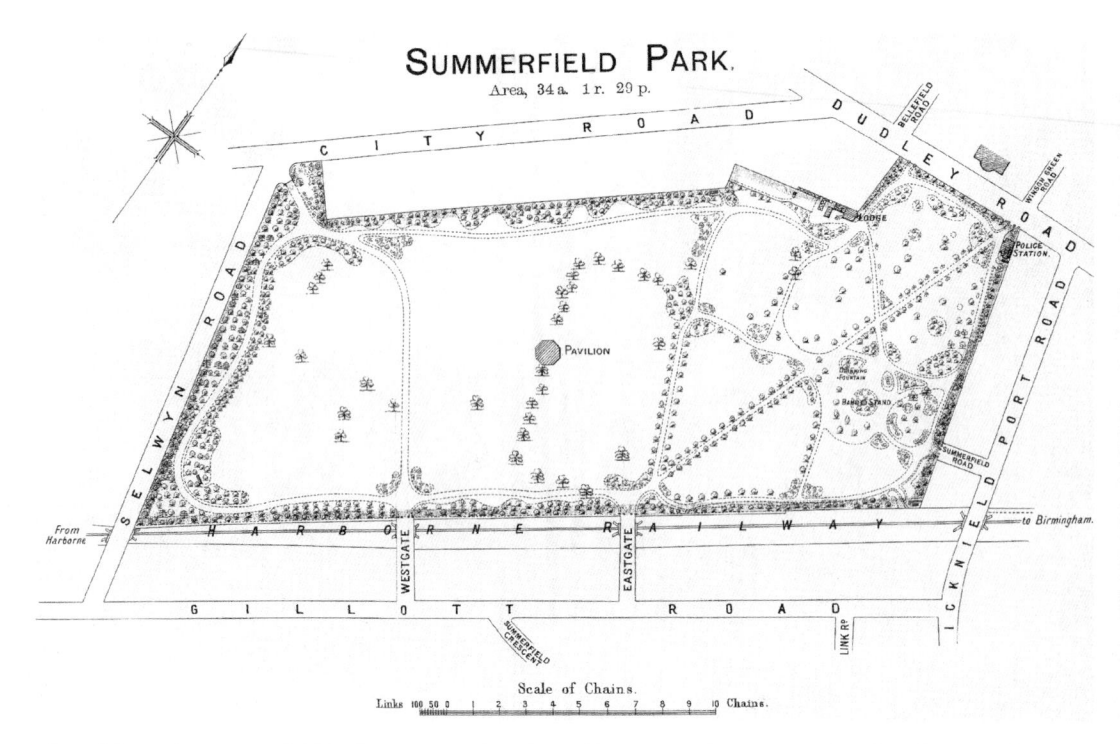

Plan of the park. Summerfield Park was opened to the public on 29 July 1876. At that date the area of the park was thirteen acres.

16

Spring Hill House. The residence of one member of the prominent Birmingham family the Galtons, it was built for John Howard Galton about 1780. It was described in *Birmingham Places* as 'a fine and large house of late Georgian style and one of the few now left of the mansions in Birmingham'. In fact there were two substantial houses on Spring Hill in the nineteenth century, the other being Spring Hill Theological College, a training centre for evangelical clergy which is commemorated in the name of College Street.

Opposite below: This cottage in Summerfield Park was part of the original Summerfield House buildings and therefore one of the very few reminders of the areas distant past still standing. It was initially used by the resident park keeper but these days it is just one of the park's outbuildings. The park itself was extended over the years 1890-1892 to thirty-four acres. At its height the park boasted numerous facilities including magnificent gardens, bowling greens, tennis courts and cricket pitches, all sadly lost in recent years due to cutbacks in spending.

The house in poor condition in 1955. It had various industrial uses. A hundred years ago the house, then called the Manor House, was the premises of R. Brown, manufacturing chemist, producing 'Real Yankee Relish' at a quarter of the price of Worcester sauce. Its most recent manifestation had been as the premises of the London Oil Corporation. The house has since been demolished.

Brown's Furniture Polish.

Bottles, 3d., 6d., and 1/-
Family Tins, 4/- and 7/6

Sold by all Grocers for **OVER FORTY YEARS.**

SEE TESTIMONIAL BELOW.

Leaves NO Fingermarks

Registered Office, Cape Hill, Smethwick, near Birmingham, Sept. 22nd, 1903.
MESSRS. RICHARD BROWN & SONS, Manufacturing Chemists, Spring Hill, Birmingham.
  GENTS—Having for some time used Brown's Furniture Polish in our Offices, likewise in our Houses for Bar Fittings, Billiard Rooms, Household Furniture, &c., we have pleasure in recommending as the best Furniture Polish we have ever used. It leaves no fingermarks and with very little labour cleans off all dirt or tarnish and leaves a brilliant and lasting polish behind to our entire satisfaction
  You may make whatever use you like of this testimonial.
    Yours faithfully, For MITCHELLS & BUTLERS, LTD., WM. BUTLER.
         CENTRAL AGENTS :
BARROW'S, Bull St. ;   **WEBSTER'S, Hagley Rd**

Richd. Brown & Sons, Manufacturing Chemists,
     Sauce, Ketchup & Pickle Works, SPRING HILL, B'HAM.
Established 1863.

Brown's produced a range of delightful products from Spring Hill House.

John Hawker's Park glass works at the top of Spring Hill, taken from Bissett's *Magnificent Directory of Birmingham*, 1808. The glass works opened in 1787, the first canal-side glass works in the town to take advantage of the transport of raw materials by canal boat.

Right: The 1845 Post Office Directory entry for Winson Green showing just how little it was built up at this date, although parts of the district also appeared under the entry for Birmingham Heath.

Winson Green, *Lodge road.*
Evans Joseph, plumber, &c
Thompson Wm. provision dealer
Winson Green, Edmund Buckley
Wilkins Joseph, butcher
Bonas John, shoemaker
Cropper Joseph, greengrocer
Cox Hiram Wm. beer retailer
Heaton Mr. Reuben (Winson cot)
Playfair Mr. Robert (Winson hill)
Stansbie Robert, shopkeeper
Preston George Green, beer retailer
Hodgetts Miss Sarah, shopkeeper
Dudley Benjamin, shoemaker
Smith Aaron, beer retailer
Spooner Mr. William
Turner James, esq. (Winson house)
Boyle Mr. James (Winson green ho)

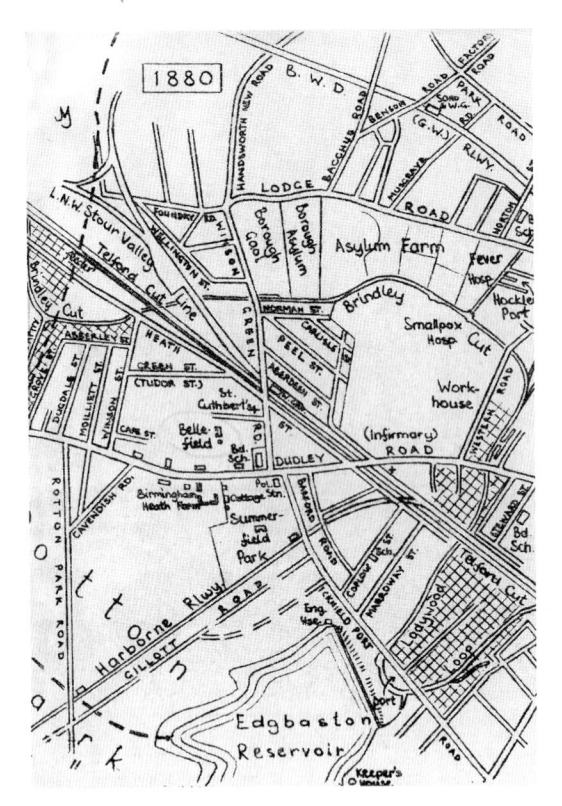

Left: An 1880 map showing the scale of building since the 1810 map.

Right: The corner of Nineveh, Park and Bacchus Roads in 1906. This junction was thought to be the site of bull baiting in the eighteenth and early nineteenth centuries. Bull baiting was apparently very popular with the workers from Matthew Boulton's Soho Manufactory. The building on the right, an off-licence advertising Holders Bottled Ales, still stands.

These two views show Musgrave Road in April 1907, shortly before the area shown here was turned into a public recreation ground.

These two views show The Black Patch on the Smethwick border, and the gypsies who frequented it up to the early years of the last century. Fond memories of the gypsy families are rooted in the history of this part of Soho.

two

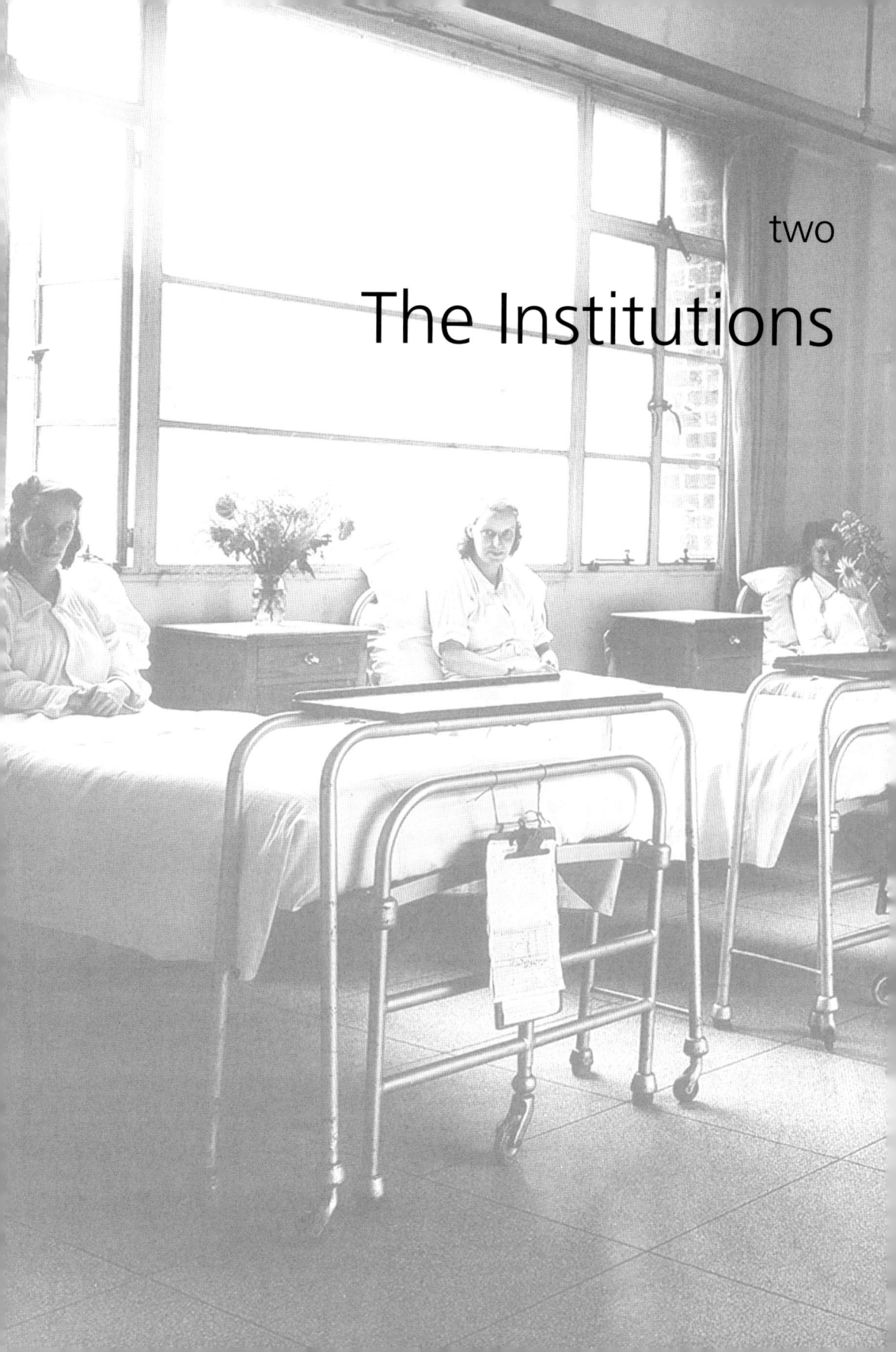

The Institutions

The front view of Winson Green Prison taken in November 1949, the year the prison celebrated its centenary. The famous and imposing gates of the prison create the look of a toy fortress. A report on poverty in Winson Green in the *Birmingham Post* made this point: 'The prison is nearby. It would look to say that it broods over the area but it does nothing of the kind. As a matter of fact it is brightness itself compared with some of the houses surrounding it.'

Winson Green was not the first prison in Birmingham. This small building in Peck Lane in the town centre, where New Street station now is, was the town's original prison but was quickly seen to be inadequate. Birmingham Heath had the space to build a suitably impressive building for the town's structure. The foundation stone was laid in 1845 and the first prisoner was accepted in Winson Green on 17 October 1849.

Above: A view along Villiers Street in 1977, with the prison gateway at the end showing just how close the nineteenth-century houses came to the gaol. Both the houses and the gateway have disappeared now.

Right: The early years of the new Winson Green prison were not happy. A Government Report in 1854 read: 'like a tenth-rate shocker, manacles, straitjackets, thrashings, tortures rivalling the Inquisition – all were being perpetrated in the name of justice and retribution.'

"TRUTH IS STRANGER THAN FICTION."

TRUE ACCOUNT

OF

HE PROCEEDINGS LEADING TO,

AND A

FULL & AUTHENTIC REPORT OF,

HE SEARCHING INQUIRY,

BY HER MAJESTY'S COMMISSIONERS,

INTO THE

HORRIBLE SYSTEM OF DISCIPLINE

PRACTISED AT THE

BOROUGH GAOL

OF BIRMINGHAM.

EDITED BY

JOSEPH ALLDAY, CHURCHWARDEN,

OF THE DEPUTATION THAT PRESENTED TO LORD PALMERSTON THE MEMORIAL ADOPTED AT A PUBLIC MEETING OF THE INHABITANTS OF BIRMINGHAM, AND WHO APPEARED, DURING THE THIRTEEN DAYS' INQUIRY, ON BEHALF OF THE MEMORIALISTS.

You have conducted yourself, Mr. Allday, throughout this Inquiry, in a most proper manner."— *Welsby, Chief Commissioner.*

'Birmingham Gaol has in secret been the scene of doings which, as they are described in the ositions of certain witnesses, have literally filled the public with horror. * * * Stories, which ld have been thought exaggerations if perused in one of Mr. Dickens' books, are now related of rough Gaol in 1853.'—*The Times, September 15th.*

BIRMINGHAM: JOHN TONKS, 85, NEW STREET;
LONDON: J. PITMAN, PATERNOSTER ROW.

PRICE ONE SHILLING.

BIRMINGHAM PRISON GATE MISSION, C.E.T.S.
WINSON GREEN, BIRMINGHAM.

President:
THE RIGHT REV. THE LORD BISHOP

Chairman:
REV. CANON COLE, M.A.,
Aston Vicarage.

Hon. Treasurer:
ALFRED PHILLIPS, ESQ.,
Glen Luce,
Jockey Road,
Sutton Coldfield.

Org. Secretary:
REV. E. RICHARDSON,
St. Simon's House,
26, South Road,
Handsworth, Birmingham.

Prison Gate Missioner:
MR. A. E. PRITCHARD,
Prison Gate Mission,
Winson Green, Birmingham.

FREEDOM! What will he become?

ONE ANSWER! See below.

The prison Gate Mission which provided an early visitor centre for families of prisoners and helped prisoners themselves on their discharge. The building is still in use opposite the gaol as a community centre.

Prisoners helping with the new building in November 1958. They also helped to build the nearby warders houses on the Winson Green Road.

Right; A warder putting up a death notice in 1955. Locals remember that when anyone was due to be hanged the road outside the prison was closed but 'not before the arrival of Mrs Van Der Elst to protest against capital punishment'.

Below: Prison Library in the 1950s. The new prison library opened in 2003 looks and feels a good deal more inviting than the one photographed here.

The new 'Lego' dome-topped prison entrance in 1989. The prison is currently expanding onto the old All Saints Hospital site.

A familiar view of the imposing structure of All Saints Hospital, previously the Lunatic Asylum. The Asylum, like the nearby prison, was designed by the same architect, D.R. Hill, who at virtually the same time was also building Birmingham's first municipal baths at Kent Street. The Asylum was completed in June 1850.

Right: The 'Rules and Regulations' of the new Asylum. This included that 'quiet patients shall be separated from those who are noisy and dangerous and the clean shall at all times be separated from the dirty'. The sexes of course were not allowed to mix. The land around the Asylum was used as a farm which supplied fresh produce to the hospital and the neighbouring prison.

PROPOSED

RULES & REGULATIONS

FOR

THE GOVERNMENT

OF THE

PAUPER LUNATIC ASYLUM

FOR THE

Borough of Birmingham,

Prepared by the Committee of Visitors thereof, pursuant to the 40th Sect. of the Act of 8 & 9 Vic. Cap. 126.

BIRMINGHAM:
PRINTED BY W. GREW AND SON, HIGH-STREET.
1850.

Left: Although innovative in its day the Asylum's original buildings proved inadequate and were condemned back in 1893. However this photograph of three schizophrenics taken in 1953 appeared in a magazine exposé of the hospital headlined 'Inside a Mental Hospital. Pictures that Will Shock Britain.'

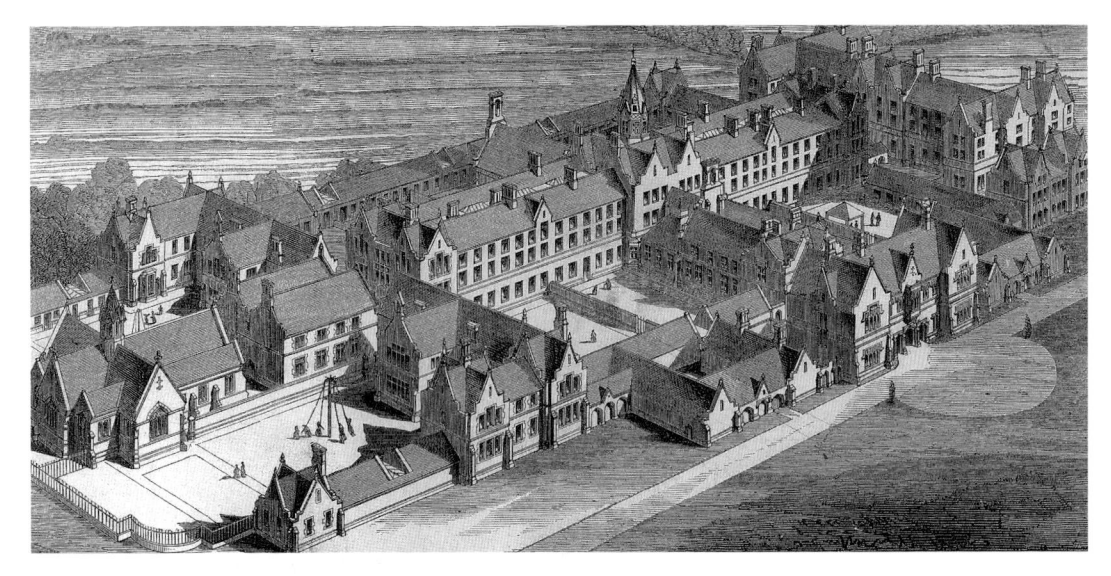

Above: The Birmingham Workhouse, designed by J.J. Bateman in a Tudor style, 1851. Before it opened in the following year 50,000 people toured the building to wonder at this latest marvel of 'the social sciences.'

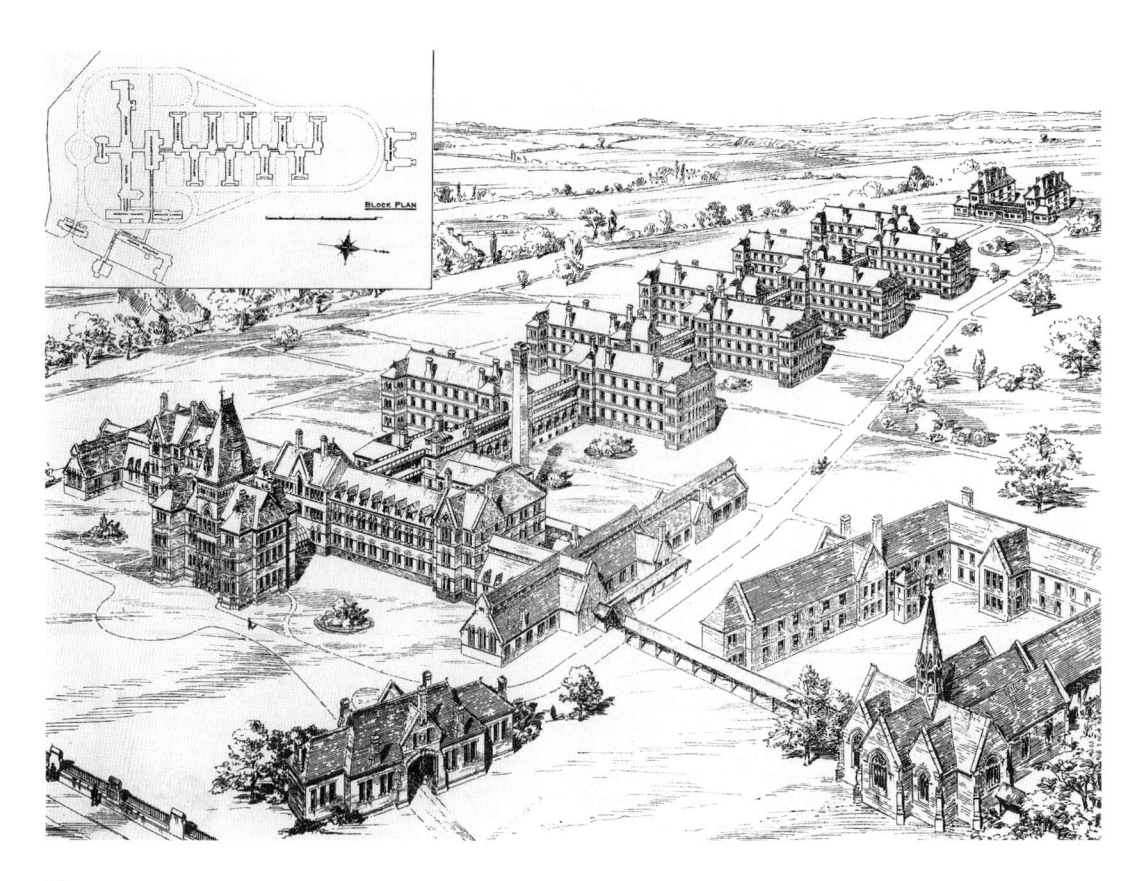

Right: The prison-like interior of the workhouse, which led it to be dubbed Birmingham's Bastille. Other names that locals gave to the workhouse were 'The Grubber', 'The House' and 'The Spike'.

Below: The workhouse building in 1959, when it was then part of Summerfield Geriatric Hospital. All but one of the Summerfield Hospital buildings have been demolished.

Opposite below: The workhouse with its new hospital buildings in 1888. The illustration appeared in the *Building News* on 3 February 1888. A reporter from *Birmingham Faces and Places* was most struck with the scale on which everything was done: 'There are the kitchens in which yesterday were prepared 3 hundredweight of meat, a hundred gallons of gruel, 3 sacks of potatoes, and 60 gallons of tea, besides 30 or 40 gallons of beef-tea'.

A postcard view of the Tower at Dudley Road Hospital, date unknown. The tower was demolished in 1964. (Andrew Maxam)

One of the exceptionally long corridors in Dudley Road Hospital.

During the First World War the hospital was used as a section of the 1st Southern General Hospital. The Birmingham Athletic Institute is here providing boxing entertainment for the recuperating soldiers.

An early hospital scene, date unknown.

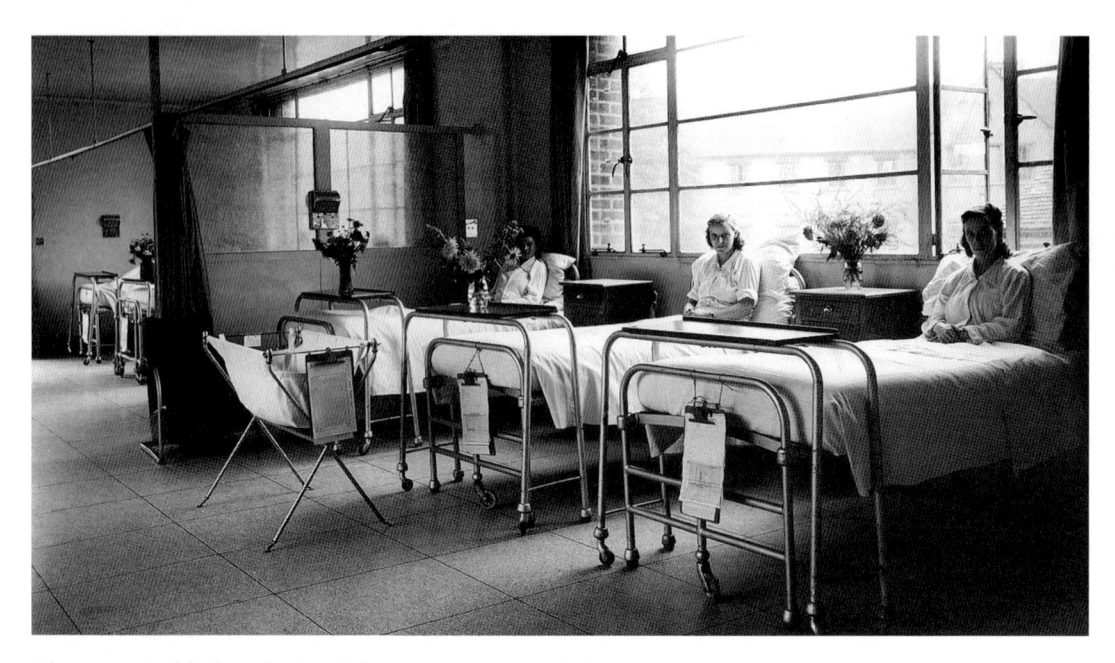

The maternity block at the hospital on 14 September 1945.

The modern-day front of the hospital from across the Dudley Road on 12 September 1968, shortly after the frontage was redesigned. Some of the old buildings are in the background.

three
Pubs

The Cape of Good Hope in 1929. The last pub on the Dudley Road before the Cape. These opened on 23 December 1925 and closed in 1995. Symptomatic of the fate of many of the pubs in this section, it has been demolished. Even worse the site is now occupied by a McDonalds, quite a climb down for such a splendid building ironically opposite the home of Mitchells and Butlers.

Two pubs on Spring Hill, both now demolished. The top photograph shows The Guild public house at No. 205 Spring Hill in 1965, sandwiched between Sheffco Tools and Files and a hairdressers. Nearer to town on the same side of the road was the Coach and Horses at No. 93, with Henry Playfair's shoe shop next door and St Peter's church behind. The Coach and Horses closed in 1970 when all of the Spring Hill shops and pubs were demolished to make way for a grassy verge.

The Great Western at the junction of Icknield Street and Park Road on 17 October 1969. It closed on 15 July 1970.

The Warstone on the corner of Icknield Street with Camden Street. It closed on 28 September 1971.

The Royal Mint, an Atkinson's pub, around 1947. The pub on the corner of Icknield and Hingeston Streets closed on 27 September 1970. At one time it had been home for the actor Tony Britton whose father was the licensee.

Mona Stores, an off-licence on the corner of Clissold and Prescott Streets in July 1968. The licensee at this date was Ethel Bennett.

The Lamb Tavern in Clissold Street, another victim of the Boulton redevelopment scheme.

A view of the Sir Charles Napier in Rosebery Street, in October 1969. (Andrew Maxam)

The Grotto public house in Camden Street, prior to demolition, in 1969.

Two pubs in Hingeston Street, The Laurels and the Brookfields Tavern. The Brookfields was at the junction of Hingeston and Pitsford Streets. This photograph dates from 18 April 1962. The Laurels, an Atkinson's pub, was on the Prescott Street corner. Both pubs fell victim to redevelopment and closed in 1970. (Andrew Maxam)

The Crown and Anchor, 39 Lodge Road. It closed on 17 August 1970. (Ted Rudge website)

One of the best remembered pubs in the area, the Hydraulic, on the corner of Lodge Road and All Saints Street. The main watering hole for workers from the Scribbans bakery works across the road. The Hydraulic closed in 1970. (Ted Rudge website)

The Don on the corner of the narrow cobbled Don Street and Lodge Road. It was a staple of the local darts and domino leagues. (Ted Rudge Website)

How Talbot Street used to look. On the extreme left-hand hand side of the photograph is The Rising Sun pub in Talbot Street, around 1908. The yard door advertises Holders Ales and Stouts.

The Talbot in Talbot Street on 31 January 1957. The pub is the only building in the road which survived redevelopment in the 1970s and still serves pints today. During the 1930s it had a large Mitchells and Butlers sign around the roof. (Andrew Maxam)

The Wonder Vault, the large white pub on the flat part of Benson Road between Bacchus Road and the railway bridge.

The Grapes on Bacchus Road in December 1956. It closed in 1992 and Vineyard Close now runs through the site of the old pub. (Andrew Maxam)

Two views of the Railway Inn at the junction of Wellington and Vittoria Streets, separated by thirty years of change. The top view is from 1971 and the lower one from 1999. (Andrew Maxam)

The Bellefield in Winson Street. Saved from demolition after a public outcry, this magnificent pub stands today in splendid isolation in Winson Street surrounded by a small park.

SAM^L. WHITE & SON,
BREWERS and BOTTLERS,
BELLEFIELD BREWERY,
WINSON GREEN, BIRMINGHAM.

Price List of Pure Home-Brewed Ales.

	QUALITY.	MARK	Pin. 4½ Galls.	Firkin. 9 Galls.	Kilderkin. 18 Galls.	Barrel. 36 Galls.	
These Ales are brewed from English Malt and Hops of the finest quality, and Pure Artesian Well Water.	MILD ALE	X	4/6	9/-	18/-	36/-	*Extract from Certificate of* William Duncan, Esq., F.I.C., F.C.S. "To summarise the results of Chemical and Microscopical Examinations, I consider that in your Deep Well supply you secure a water of maximum purity and excellent quality for the production of sound competition Ales and Beers."
	,, ,,	XX	5/3	10/6	21/-	42/-	
	,, ,,	XXX	6/-	12/-	24/-	48/-	
	STRONG ALE	XXXX	7/6	15/-	30/-	60/-	
	LIGHT BITTER	FA	4/6	9/-	18/-	36/-	
	,, ,,	LB	5/3	10/6	21/-	42/-	
	BEST BITTER	PA	6/-	12/0	24/-	48/-	

LIBERAL DISCOUNT FOR CASH.

List of Bottled Goods.

	DESCRIPTION.	
BOTTLED AT THE BREWERY.	GUINNESS' EXTRA STOUT, Reputed Pints ,, ,, ,, Half Pints "EMPIRE" PALE ALE - - Half Pints SYPHONS OF SODA WATER "SANTÉ" MINERAL WATERS	ALL ORDERS RECEIVE PROMPT ATTENTION.

TERMS:—Strictly Net. Cash on Delivery.

TELEPHONE: Central No. 1147.

Left: This advertisement for White's brewery dates from 1911. Samuel White sold beer here from about 1888 and in 1897 he began brewing. The brewery eventually closed after it and the pub was taken over by Davenports in 1952.

Right: The magnificent interior in March 1975, 'one of the best and snuggest pub rooms in Birmingham'. The gem inside is the smoke room with its floor to ceiling dark green tiles.

Two views of The Albion at No. 187 Heath Street. It closed along with its neighbour the Heath Street Tavern when Heath Street was re-developed in the '70s. (Andrew Maxam). The lower photograph shows the building on its last legs on 26 April 1977.

The annual anniversary parade from Cromwell Hall mission gather outside the Malt Shovel in Tudor Street in June 1958. (Irene Lockwood)

The Oak at No. 77 Lansdowne Street on 13 May 1977, just prior to its demolition. (Andrew Maxam)

Above: The Cape of Good Hope in 1901. The Cape was opposite another Mitchells and Butlers pub, the Locomotive Engine. They had different closing hours which led to mad scrambles across the road to get in a last pint.

Above: The old building was replaced by this impressive Mitchells and Butlers pub. It is shown here in 1939 with tramcar number 124 working on the 55 route.

Opposite below: The Duke of Edinburgh on the Dudley Road, photographed in June 1973.

The smoke room in the Cape. This illustration appears in *Fifty Years of Brewing, 1879-1929*, a history of the brewers Mitchells and Butlers.

The forecourt of the Old Windmill on the Dudley Road, also in June 1973. The name celebrates the windmill which used to stand on Birmingham Heath perhaps a few hundred yards from the present building. The Old Windmill, along with the Wheatsheaf and the Birmingham Arms, still serves the needs of local drinkers on this small section of the Dudley Road.

Lee Bridge Tavern taken from a photograph in 1921, two years after the pub opened. This splendid building, the last of the main Dudley Road pubs to be built, is sadly disused at the moment and has been for about seven years. (Andrew Maxam)

four
Churches and Schools

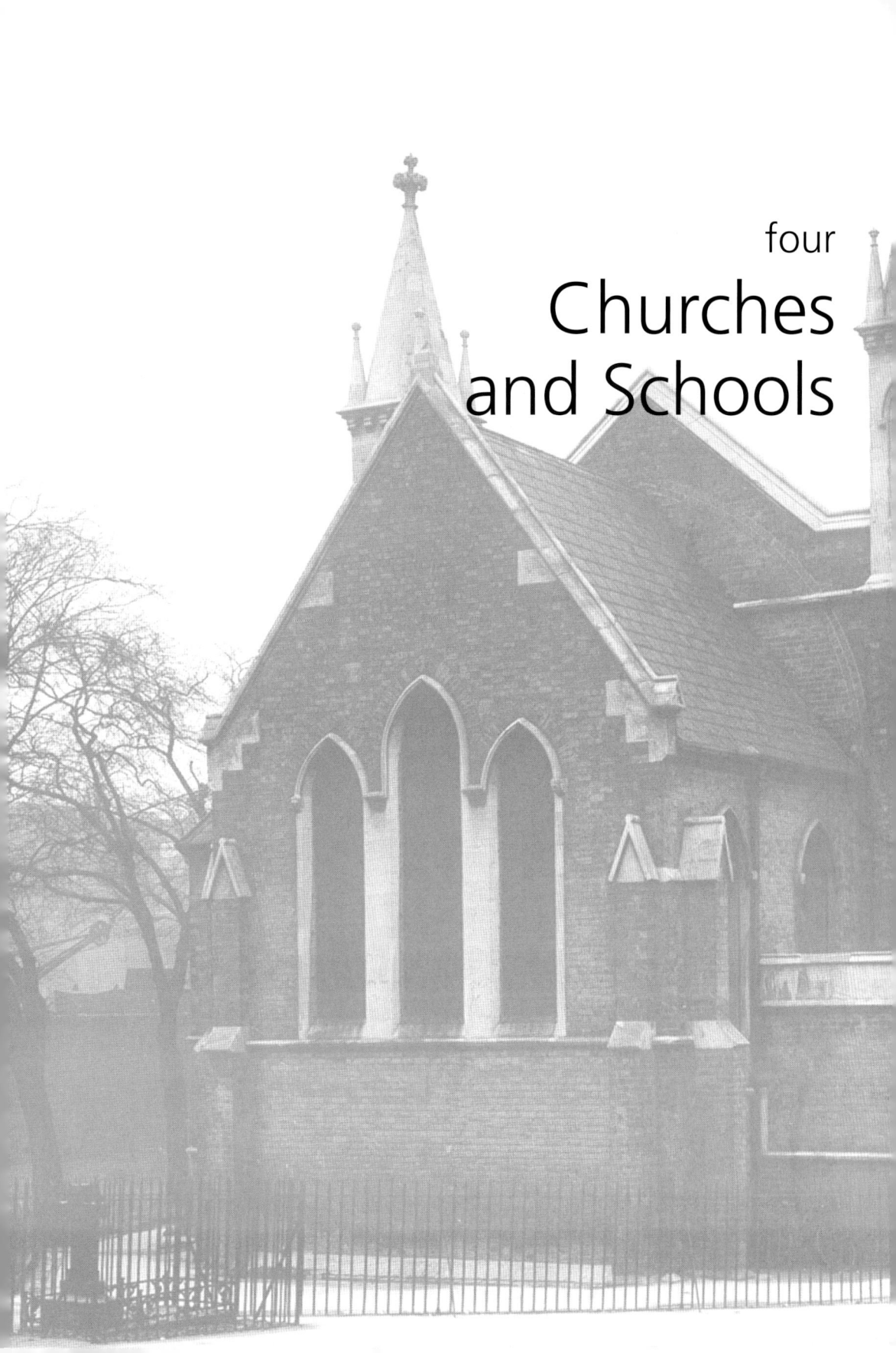

First Communion group at St Patrick's Catholic church on the Dudley Road in June 1953. The group are photographed outside the priest's house.

Two views of St Chrystoms church at the Musgrave corner of Dover and Park Streets in 1973. Opened in 1885 as a mission church of All Saints it was consecrated in 1889. It is a building of brick stone facings designed by John Cotton in the early English style. Even by the 1950s the church's best was behind it and one local remembers 'a rough old church, I cannot think of worse surroundings than that church had, the corrugated metal façade of the timber yard opposite, scrap yards and derelict land with old metal and wood fencing alongside and a railway bridge fifty yards away – a scene of sheer beauty. If we had had our way we would have married at St Michaels' (this was at the top of the hill).

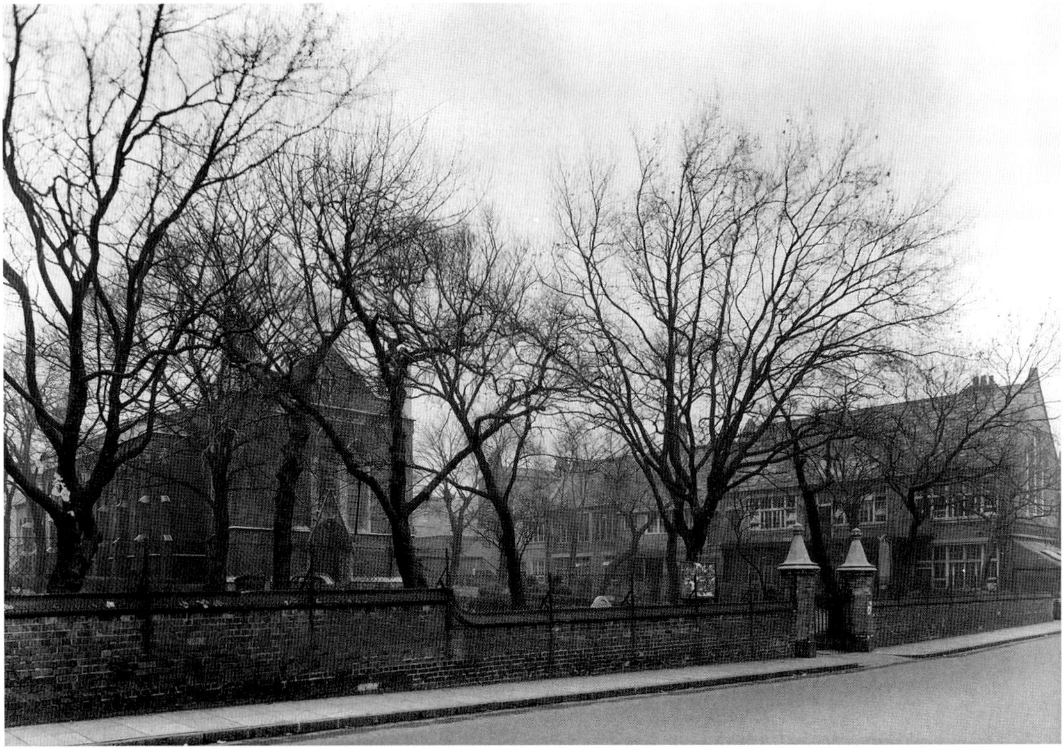

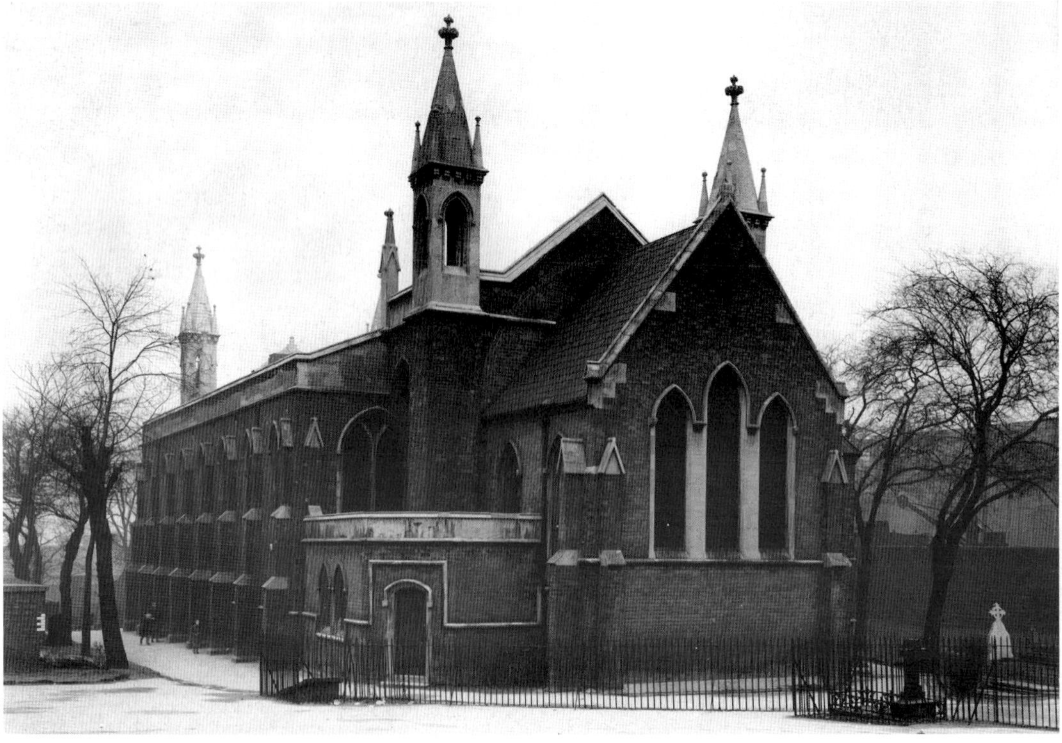

Four views of All Saints Church, Hockley, in 1973. It was by some way the first church in the district, being consecrated on 28 September 1833. The building was designed by Rickman and Hutchinson and built in red brick in the Gothic style. At one time it was by far the largest parish in Birmingham with a potential congregation of 30,000 by the 1880s, including the hospitals and the prison.

With the coming of the railway the church found itself sandwiched between the Great Western mainline and the Hockley Goods Yard. By the late 1950s the congregation was pathetically small and the building itself in a dangerous state. It staggered on for a few more years before demolition.

Above: The Methodist church in New Spring Street. It was built in 1893 by the Methodist New Connexion for the Crabtree Road congregation. It is now the New Testament church of God in Brookfields.

Left: St Cuthberts. The church was built in 1871; the foundation stone being laid by Lord Leigh with full Masonic rites. Part of the parish was taken away to form part of the parish of Bishop Latimer in 1904. The building itself was crumbling away by the thirties and the vicar took out an advertisement in the *Birmingham Mail* in 1934 appealing for £800 to save the church. In the 1930s the vicar, the Revd Bothwell-Botton, was well known in the community for his work for destitute men. His work for the free night shelter in Winson Green Road was 'as fine a piece of practical Christianity as one could imagine.'

Winson Green Congregational church at the corner of Villiers Street and Winson Green Road in June 1972, prior to its demolition. The church was built in 1882 on the site of an earlier mission hall, and within ten years it had a congregation of 300. By 1957 this was down to sixty – a familiar story for most Winson Green and Brookfields churches and chapels.

Above: The engagement party for Leonard Hawksworth and Irene Thompson at St Cuthbert's church hall, December 1941. (Janet Ingram)

Opposite above: Despite the impression given in this photograph, St Cuthbert's was one of the poorest parishes in Birmingham. Even in the 1930s the church struggled with the twin evils of poverty and unemployment. Parishioners moved out from the crowded back-to-backs to the outer suburbs, leaving an even more deprived congregation. Except on special occasions no collections were taken during the services as 'a discreet recognition of the poverty of the congregation'. (Janet Ingram)

Opposite below: The wartime wedding of Leonard Hawksworth and Irene Thompson at St Cuthbert's church on 20 February 1943. (Janet Ingram)

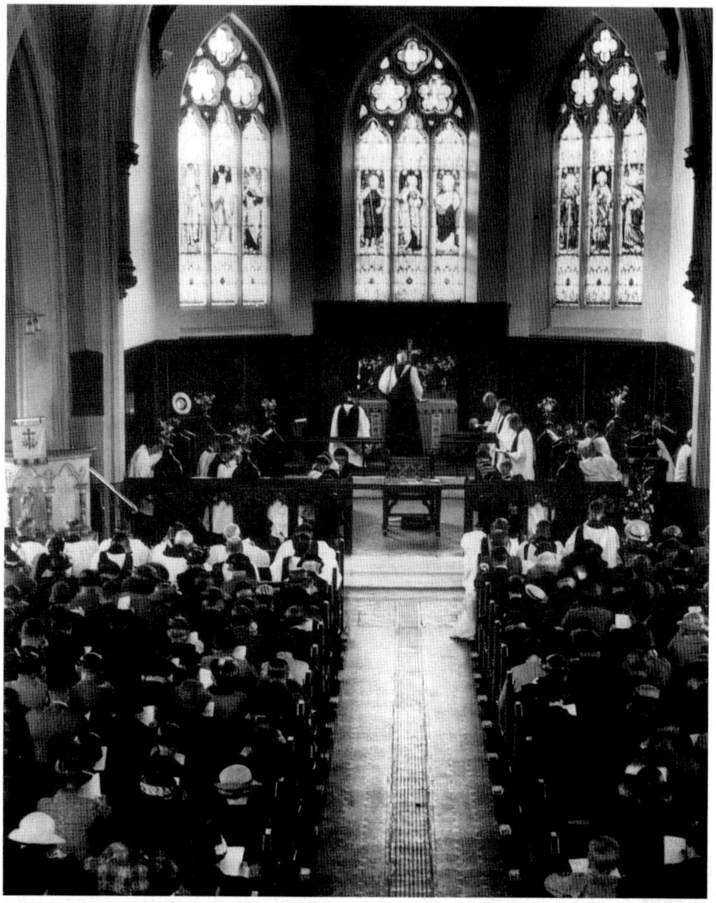

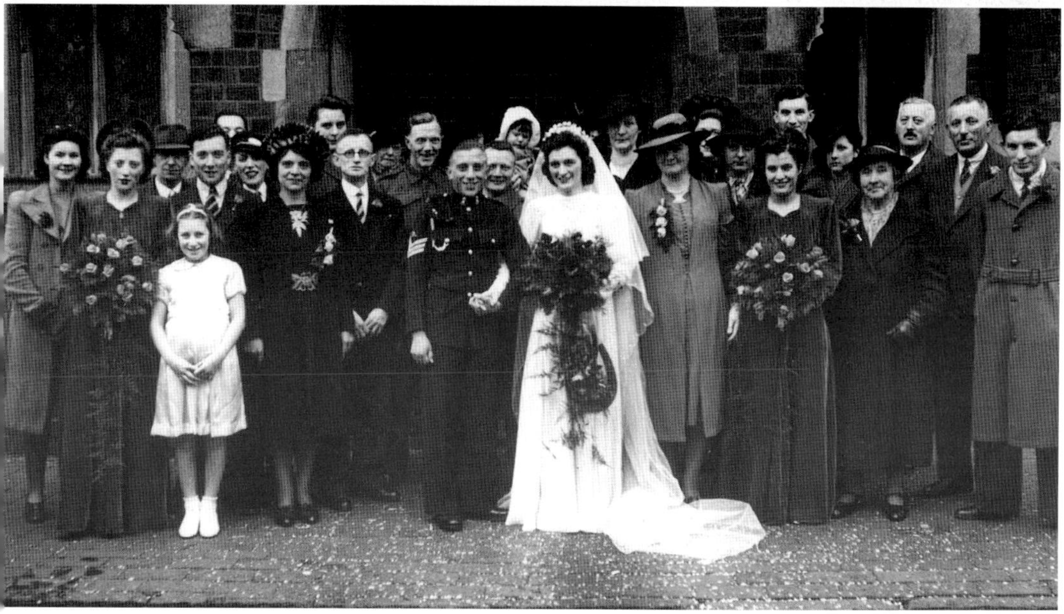

Above: Bishop Latimer church on the Handsworth New Road in March 1987. A Grade-II Listed building, it was designed by the architect W.H. Bidlake and built in 1903/4. The listed description compares the church to an East Anglian Perpendicular wool church with a very high quality use of stone and brick typical of Bidlake's attention to detail.

Left: An early postcard view of St Patrick's Roman Catholic church on the Dudley Road. The card was posted in 1908. A Grade-II Listed building built between 1876 and 1895 it was opened by Bishop Ilsley on 29 October 1895. Along with the St Patrick's school the church continues to act as a focal point for the local Catholic community.

Opposite below: Lodge Road Pentecostal church. It was opened in 1860, replaced in 1868 and renovated in 1902. It was severely damaged in the Second World War and in 1954 was sold to the Assemblies of God.

A postcard view of Spring Hill Baptist chapel. The chapel was built in 1886 at a cost of £3,200. In 1892 there was a Sunday evening congregation of 235.

Cromwell Hall in Heath Green Road in 1901. The independent mission hall was built in 1894 and was originally known as Park Hall. It was bought in 1896 by the well-known evangelist Thomas Hope Aston *(below)* of the Christian Evidence and Protestant Layman's Association and the hall's name was changed. (Joyce Lockwood)

The interior of Cromwell Hall. The hall was demolished in 1997 and two new houses, numbers 24 and 26, were built in its place. (Joyce Lockwood)

Sunday school children from Cromwell Hall processing down Heath Green Road in around 1959. The mission hall can just be seen in the recess on the left-hand side of the road. (Joyce Lockwood)

All Saints School. The school opened in 1844. Looking rather the worse for age, the building is still in use but not as a school, it is currently used by the Young Offenders Team.

Benson Road School in October 1961. The school opened in 1888 for 962 pupils. It is still used as an Infants and Junior school, although is now called Benson Community School. It now has about 300 pupils, four-fifths of whom come from homes where English is not the first language.

Handsworth New Road School in 1977. Listed as a Grade-II building, it opened in 1901 for 1,100 pupils and is the only secondary school in the area. The building was enlarged by Birmingham Education Committee before the Great War to provide space for children up to the age of fourteen.

BIRMINGHAM F.C.

F.A. CUP FINALISTS, 1930-1931

Presented by THE BIRMINGHAM GAZETTE

Mr A. L. KNIGHTON	CROSBIE J.	MORRALL G.	HIBBS H.	LESLIE A.	CURTIS E.	A TAYLOR
MANAGER						TRAINER
	CRINGAN J.	BRIGGS G.	BRADFORD J.	BARKAS E.	FIRTH J.	GREGG R.
		ON GROUND — LIDDELL G.	HORSMAN W.			

George Liddell, Head Teacher at Handsworth New Road in the 1950s, photographed during his playing days with Birmingham City. He played as a wing half and full back from 1920 to 1932 and a year later became manager, serving until May 1939.

70

Above left and right: Pupils from Norton Street School in 1894. The Local Studies section of the Central Library has another six of these unnamed portraits of late-Victorian scholars. Norton Street Board School opened in 1876 and closed in 1932 when the pupils transferred to Benson Road. Pupils at Benson Road in the 1950s recall that their school books were stamped 'Norton Street'.

Opposite above: Icknield Street School in August 1972. It opened in 1883 for 870 pupils. Although just outside the area of this book many local children went there. It is a Grade II-Listed building now urgently in need of restoration.

Opposite below: An art lesson at Icknield Street School in 1896.

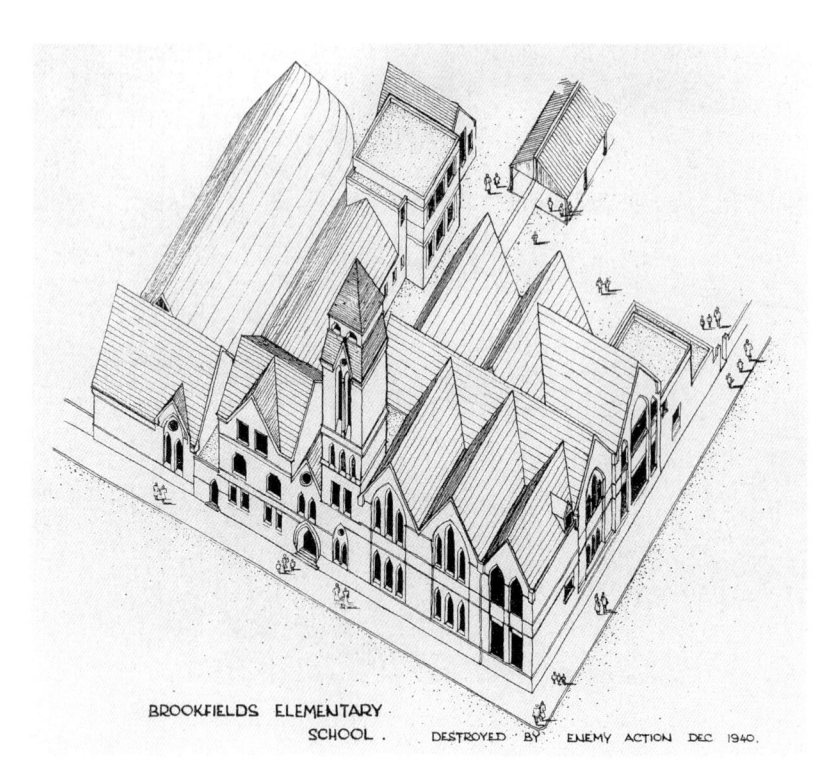

BROOKFIELDS ELEMENTARY SCHOOL. DESTROYED BY ENEMY ACTION DEC 1940.

Ellen Street School, which was destroyed by enemy action in the war. It was originally built in 1877 for 1,018 pupils.

Brookfields School, which replaced Ellen Street, was formally opened on 28 October 1950 by the then Minister of Education, G. Tomlinson. The site was extended from the original school site to include the area of surrounding houses also destroyed by a landmine.

Camden Street School, one of the Board schools. Built in 1890 for 1,090 pupils it has since been demolished. This school group is from 1950.

Foundry Road Junior and Infant School, originally Foundry Road Board School, which opened its doors back in 1883. It was built to accommodate about 1,000 children.

A recent view of Summerfield Community Centre, in a previous life Dudley Road Board School. The original school opened in 1878 with accommodation for over 1,200 pupils.

St Patrick's Catholic School, group photograph from 1953. From left to right, back row: Eddie Clements, Raymond Lawton, Joan Evans, Pat Badger, ? McGuire, Vera Dunmore, Georgina ?, ? McMarthy, Margaret Storey, Irene Parsons, Denise Austin, Peter Hatch, Billy Betham. Third row: Alan Hanson, David Bogan, Michael Mahon, Gillian Williams, Collen Donovan, Josephine Wheeler, Gillian Huff, Coleen Hayward, Mary Teirnen, Michael Curran, Paul Dashy, Francis Whelan. Second row: Adrian McNulty, John Seal, Michael Burns, Theresa Foster, Beryl Windsor, Barbara Gaffney, Miss Power, Mary Sherry, Bridie Murphy, Gerald Perkins, Michael Windsor, Joan Tighe. Front row: Michael Austin, Sean Flynn, Peter Davis, Roger Deely, Dennis Freeze, John Myatt, Bernard Gallacher, John Burke, David Cooper. (Francis Whelan)

five
Shopping on the Dudley Road and the Flat

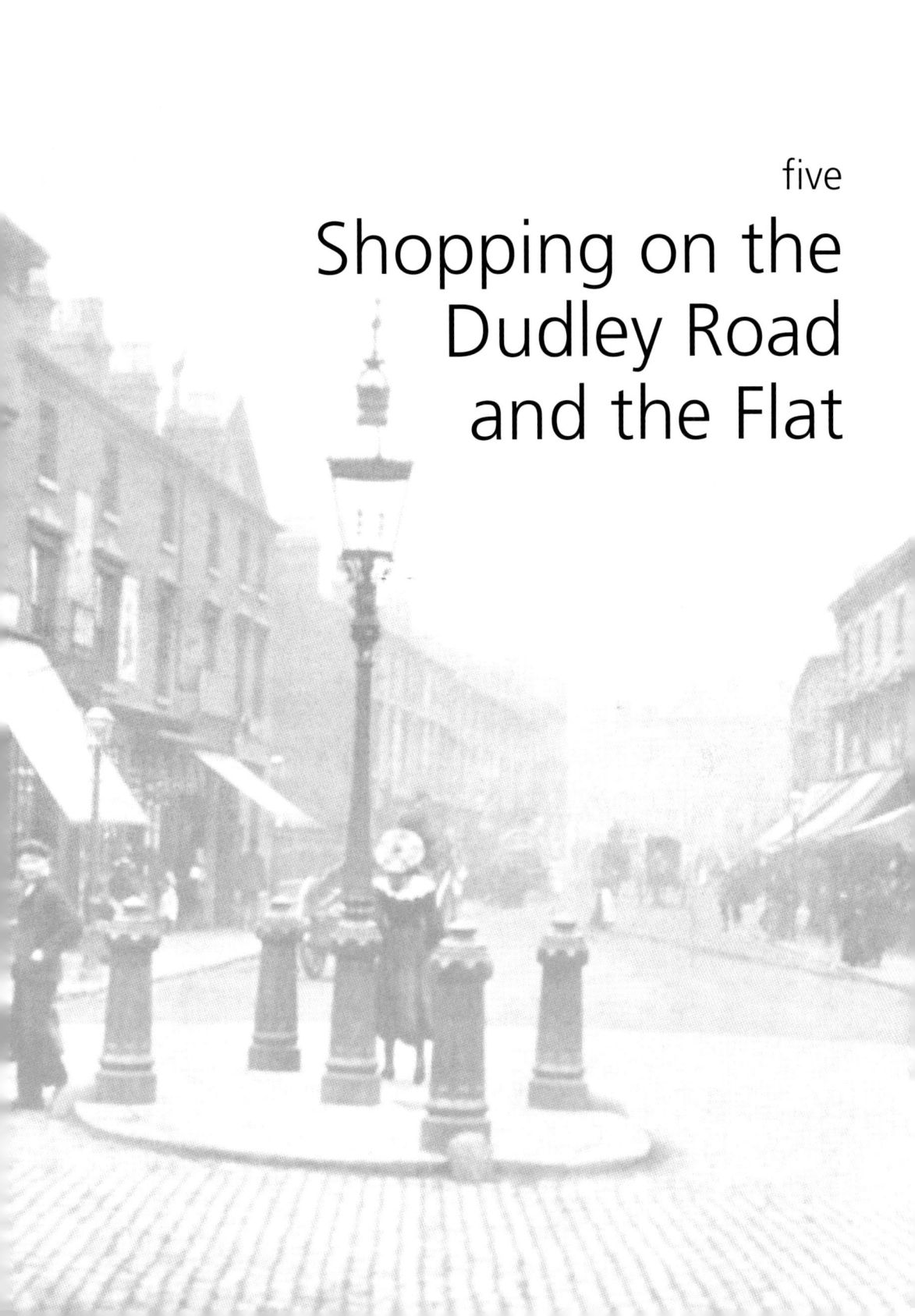

West Birmingham Market shops, between Chiswell and Winson Streets, on 9 May 1960. Next to Westlake's garage was the confectioners, Yapp & Sons. The block was built as a prestige shopping development in 1895. This block of shops is virtually unrecognizable today

Woodcock's the tobacconists between the Birmingham Arms pub and the Western café, at No. 40 Dudley Road, September 1968.

Numbers 52-54 Dudley Road, June 1973. These shops have since been pulled down and the land has not been built on. Davis's sign had been there since the twenties. In the mid-eighties a plan to turn the Dudley Road into a dual carriageway to act as the main radial route into the city from the north-west was defeated by pressure from residents and traders. The Dudley Road is still an important shopping centre for the residents of Winson Green and Brookfields.

A short section of the Dudley Road in August 1980. The Old Windmill pub is the recessed building next to the Birmingham Typewriter Centre.

Numbers 126-130 Dudley Road in September 1968. No. 130 was J. Hammond's newsagents. The buildings were put up in 1873 and 1874 just before the construction of back-to-backs was banned in Birmingham. The Birmingham City Council commissioned a survey of the group of back-to-back houses at numbers 120-132 Dudley Road in 1999, just prior to the demolition of the block. A copy of the survey, which includes a number of interior photographs, is kept in Birmingham Central Library.

No. 244 Dudley Road in November 1975. The block just past Summerfield Park on the way out of town is still standing, and No. 244 still bears the signs for Jones's as well as one of the previous owners, Bennetts. The small terrace behind the shop still stands.

No. 383 Dudley Road at the corner with Winson Street, with Julie's ladies outfitters behind the lorry, sometime in the 1970s. On the opposite corner was, and still is, The Yorkshire Grey pub.

The block of shops from Winson Street down to Moillet Street, numbers 383-437 Dudley Road, showing the changing face of the shops in the seventies.

Above: Lloyd's Bank on the corner with City Road shortly after it opened. The building is just about to celebrate its centenary. It was the only bank in the whole area and even then mostly served Rotton Park and Edgbaston. In fact Lloyds pulled out in 1987 and the building is currently used by Summerfield Foundation helping the regeneration and development of the community, including operating the Rotton Park and Winson Green Credit Union. Plans are in hand to modernise the interior which today still looks as it did a century ago *(below)*.

Right: Jack Jesson and his wife Clara outside their confectioners shop at No. 447 Dudley Road, around 1981. Jack was for many years the organist at the nearby Cromwell Hall Mission church in Heath Green Road. (Irene Lockwood).

Below: Birmingham Co-op branch 129 at No. 153 Dudley Road, date unknown. This was only a small branch, the main one on the Dudley road was on the other side at numbers 264-276. (Birmingham Co-op History Group)

UNCLE McKIE
THE PAWNBROKER,
186 & 188, DUDLEY ROAD.

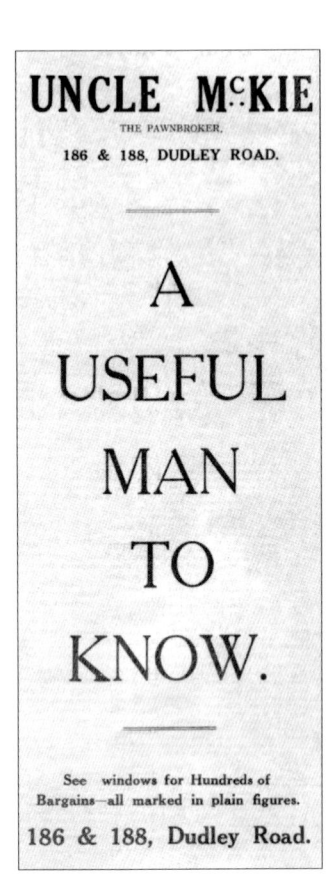

A USEFUL MAN TO KNOW.

See windows for Hundreds of Bargains—all marked in plain figures.

186 & 188, Dudley Road.

Left: This advertisement is taken from the *Dudley Road News*, a short-lived newspaper produced by the Dudley Road Tradesmen's Committee in 1925. The Committee's aim was to make Dudley Road the premier shopping road in the city.

Below: Early days on the Flat before the First World War, when children would play at Lodge Road/Icknield Street junction, and notice the photographer. Freeman, Hardy and Willis were already there selling their shoes and opposite was a hairdressers and The Grimsby fish restaurant.

Above: Looking down the Flat from Park Road towards Key Hill and the Bulls Head in 1977. It was virtually the last days of the Flat as a major shopping centre.

Below: Numbers 383-389 Lodge Road, which included George's Milk Bar, a mecca for teenagers in the 1950s and '60s. 'All we ever wanted was enough money for a bottle of coke and some tanners to put in the juke box'. (website)

One of the best-remembered shops on the Flat was Harry Spencer's greengrocers, which always seemed to have chickens and rabbits hanging up and fish on a slab. Mytton's the butchers was next door and best remembered for slaughtering live animals. Sheep and cattle arrived by cattle truck, the road was blocked off and the animals led down an alley to be slaughtered at the rear of the shop. The occasional animal escaped, bringing a touch of the countryside to this most urban of settings.

Pope's gentlemen's outfitters at No. 6 Lodge Road, next door to George Mason's grocers and Glarry's in the sixties. The proprietor of Popes was remembered as a real gentleman, selling bow ties and being a 'bit upmarket'.

One of the numerous Birmingham Co-op branches, this one is branch 80 at numbers 15-17 Lodge Road, photographed around 1950. (Birmingham Co-op History Group)

A constant on the Flat; Freeman, Hardy and Willis's shoe shop.

Above: The view from the Flat looking up Key Hill, with Norton's department store on the corner. The Flat now consists of the truncated part of Lodge Road from Heaton Street to Ford Street comprising numbers 15-30 and 380-405. Of the old shops only H.V. Smith's bakery survives.

Below: Douro's wine shop on the corner of the Flat and Ford Street. The police box is still evident at this time.

Right: Directory entry for the north side of Lodge Road, showing the shops on that side of the Flat in 1959.

LODGE RD. Hockley (18), 268 Icknield st. to H.M. Prison, Winson Green rd. Map D 1, D 2, E 2, F 2.

NORTH SIDE.
1 Pooles Central Warehouse Ltd. house furnishers
2 & 3 Freeman, Hardy & Willis Limited, boot & shoe mkrs
4 Alan's (B'ham) Ltd. soft furnishings
5 Glarry's Gown Shop Ltd. gowns
6 Pope S. gents' outfitter
7 Mason George J.Limited, grocers
9 Harris Joseph Ltd. dyers & cleaners
10 Blindells W. B. S. Ltd. boot & shoe mkrs. & dlrs
11 Gee Mrs. Alice, china dlr
12 & 28 Burley's (H. Hall), butcher
13 Scrivens Ltd. opticians
14 Boots The Chemists
...... *here is Heaton st* ......
15, 16 & 17 Birmingham Co-operative Society Ltd
18 Marsh & Baxter Ltd.ham & bacon curers
19 Melias Ltd. food distributors
19A Hudson Arth. H.butchr
20 Hudson Mrs. L. draper
21 Woolley Miss Doris, confectioner
22, 23 & 24 Spencer H. (Fruiterers) Ltd. greengrocers
25 Mytton J. E. Ltd. butchers
26 Hunt James (Bakers) Ltd
27 Pearks Dairies Ltd. provision dlrs
28 & 12 Burley's (H. Hall), butcher
29 Playfair Henry Ltd. boot & shoe dlrs
30 Douro Wine Shops Ltd. wine & spirit dlrs
here are Ford st. & Park rd

# The Workplace

six

A balloon view of Barker and Allen's Nickel Silver Rolling Mills at the top of Spring Hill, which replaced the earlier glassworks in about 1904. This illustration comes from the *Birmingham Magazine of Arts and Industries*.

The Heath Street South site of Earle, Bourne & Co. just off the Dudley Road. This view has changed very little over the years.

The main entrance to the offices. Again this is very recognisable today even if the fine doors have been replaced. The company became part of Delta Metals in the 1960s but is now owned by Fred and Denis Eastwood and leased back to E.I.P. Metals Ltd.

The workers canteen. Nowadays such distinctions have gone and the workforce drastically reduced.

The canteen kitchen.

The general offices. Probably less paper in evidence than current 'paperless' offices!

The general manager's office, now the Managing Director's office. The painting on the wall still exists.

What the factory was and is all about – the production of steel. The photograph shows the no. 1 rolling mill.

"A Tribute to all those

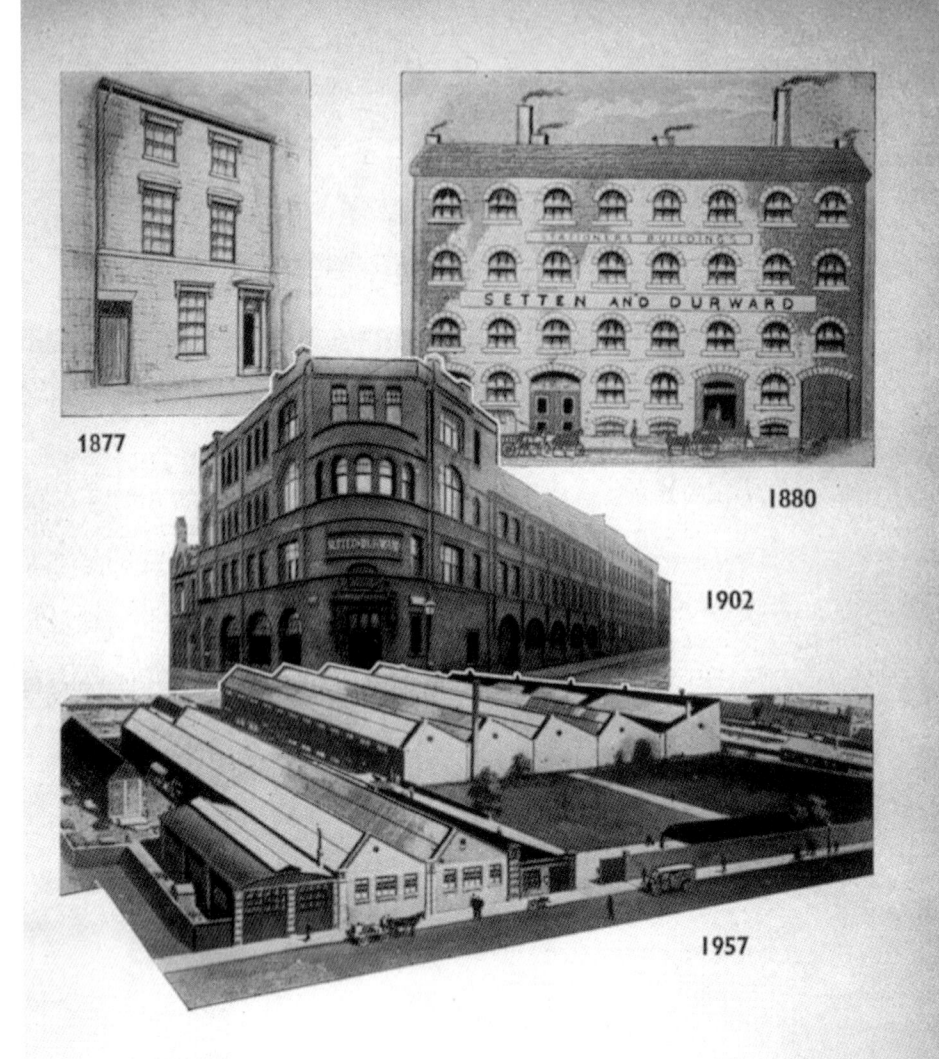

1877

1880

1902

1957

Past & Present"

who have given loyal service, and to all friends who have helped us to gain the success we have achieved in our eighty years endeavour.

These illustrations show the various premises that the firm has occupied, at the present date the large ground floor factory in Benson Road, twice extended since 1945, is hardly sufficient for its needs.

Above: Two views of the most recent premises of Settern & Durward, the Criterion Works, in Benson Road. The firm closed in the 1960s.

Opposite: The various premises of Settern & Durward Ltd, one of the main employers in the area. The company made a range of stationery equipment.

Left: Nettlefold's was one of the main employers in the district. Some form of metal bashing probably employed the most number of workers from the area.

93

Meredith & Co. on Western Road, November 1961.

R. White's soft drink manufacturers on the Western Road, November 1961.

ALWAYS ASK FOR

R. WHITE'S
MINERAL WATERS

Largest Sale in the World.

"OLD STYLE" GINGER BEER,
KAOLA, LIME JUICE & SODA,
LEMONADE, etc.

DRINK

"ZESTO"
STIMULATING & SATISFYING.

R. WHITE & SONS, LTD.,
WESTERN ROAD, BIRMINGHAM.
Telephone: NORthern 1580

An advertisement for R. White's mineral waters.

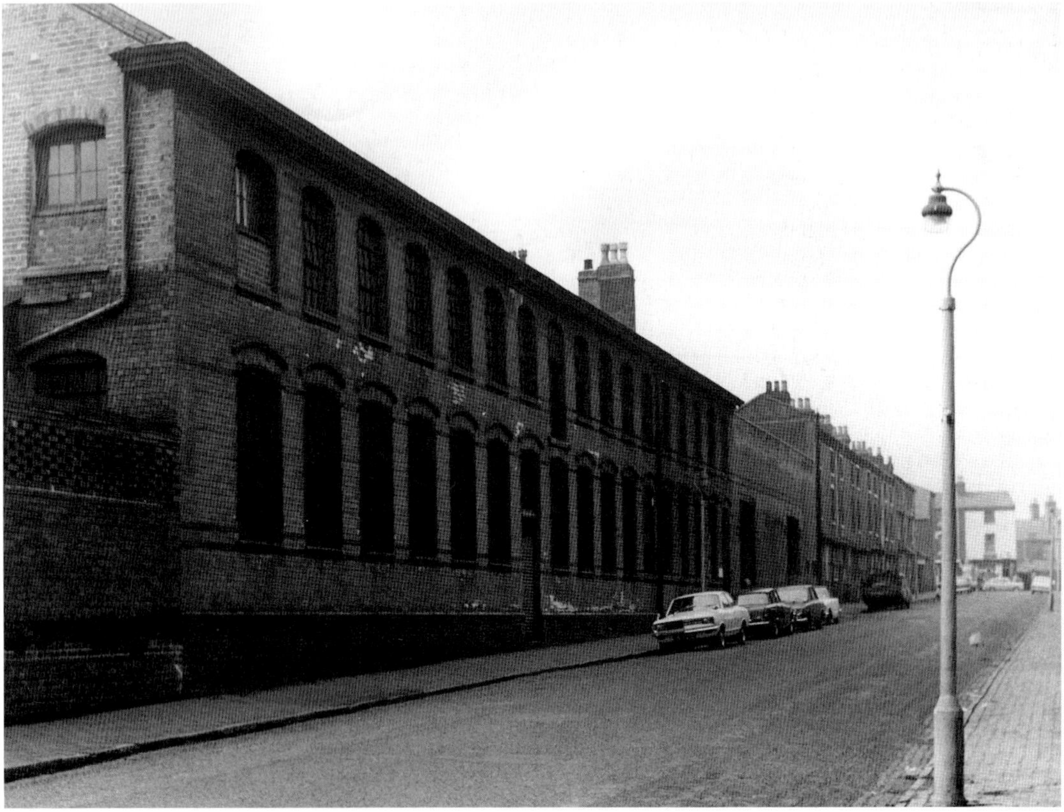

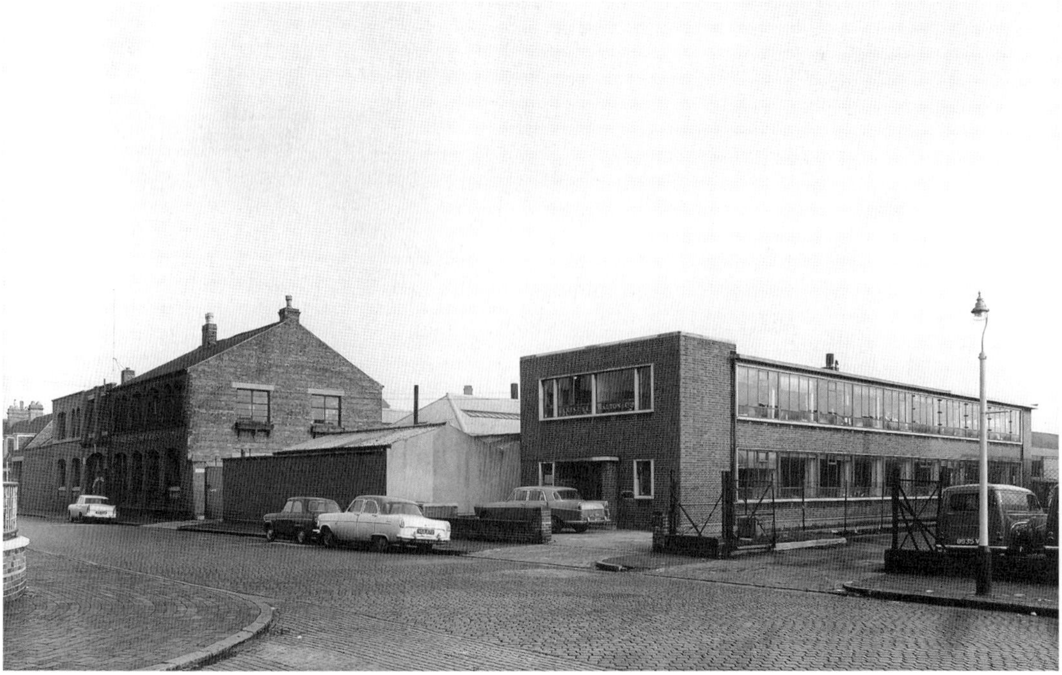

Above: Clissold Foundry, an iron foundry at No. 117 Spring Hill, between George Street West and College Street.

Opposite above: Sutton and Ash, iron and steel stockholders in New Spring Street.

Opposite below: Bannister, Walton & Co., constructional engineers based in Western Road, November 1961.

Above: Winson Green maltings for the brewers Mitchells and Butlers.

Left: Scribbans bakery, 'The Home of Purity Bread', in Goode Street. Situated just over the border in Hockley, it has been included because many Winson Green and Brookfields residents worked there and because the building itself was such a local landmark with its lightning conductor on the roof. It was demolished in the sixties.

seven

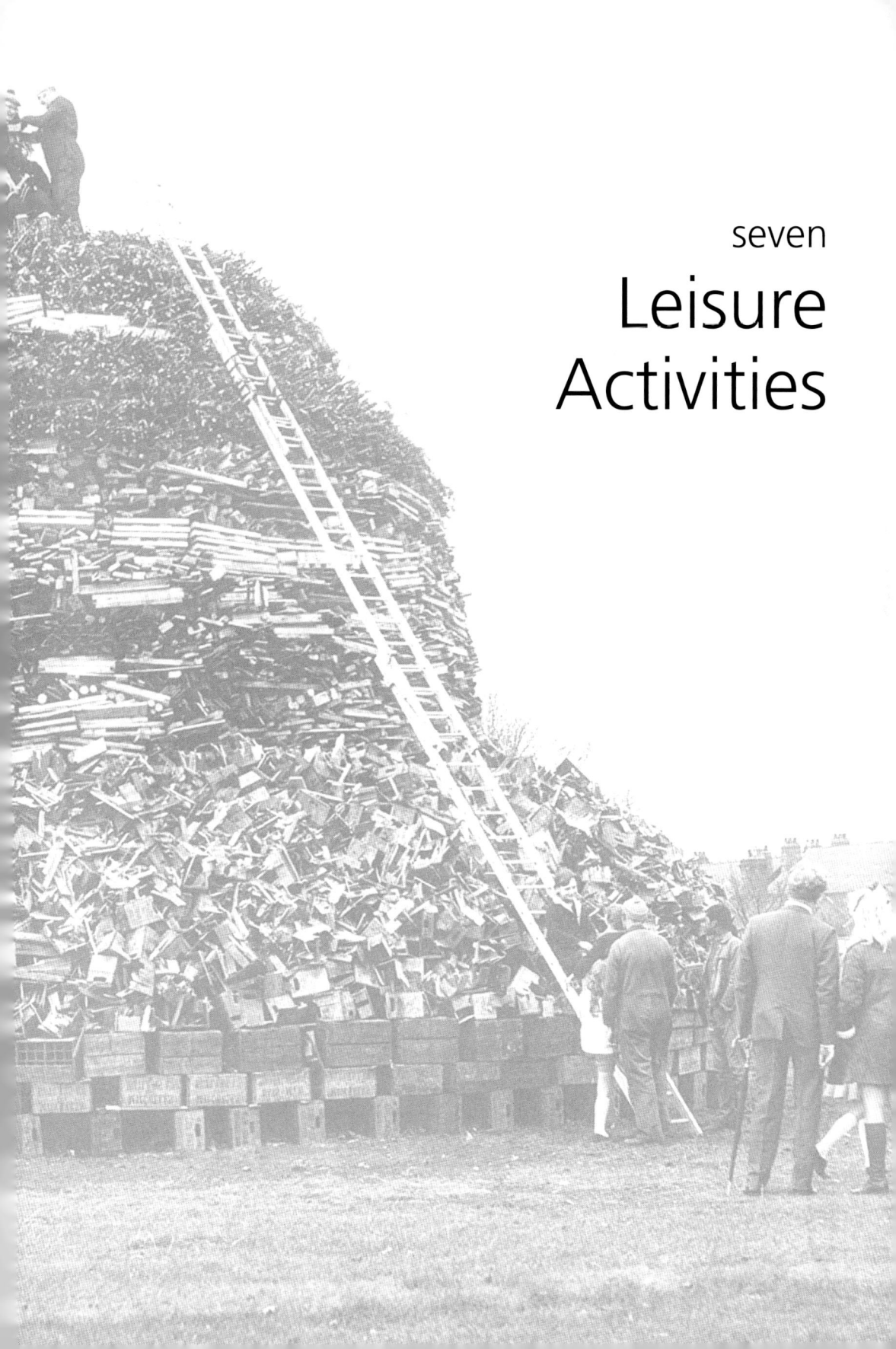

Leisure
Activities

Left: A lunchtime break for the staff of Earle, Bourne & Co. spent on the roof of the main office buildings.

Below: Summerfield Park bandstand on a Sunday afternoon, 15 July 1906. Listening to the band of HM Guards. A new bandstand, which still stands but is in rather a neglected state, replaced this bandstand in 1907.

A postcard view of local soccer team Winson Green United during the 1911/12 season. Junior soccer flourished in the area at this date. There was a Winson Green League featuring teams such as Benson United, Nineveh Wesleyan, City Road Old Boys and Bearwood Unity. Games were played at Summerfield Park. Hockley Abbey played in the Birmingham Works League while among teams seeking friendly games through the columns of the *Sports Argus* were Winson Green Congregationals and Bacchhus Ivydale. (Andrew Maxam)

Preparing for Guy Fawkes night in Summerfield Park in 1970. The city used to have an annual bonfire in Summerfield Park but this has not happened in recent years. In its heyday the park boasted an open air theatre, a Sons of Rest clubhouse, bowling and putting greens and prize-winning gardens, all of which have been lost over the years as cutbacks have affected the look of the city's parks.

Black Patch Park in November 1981. After the gypsies left the wasteland it was converted into a public park – one of the few areas of greenery in the district. It holds many memories of childhood escapades for former residents of Winson Green. The parkie 'Padgett' is well remembered with 'his gleaming boots crunching the gravel underfoot, his smart black uniform and peaked hat marking his omnipotent presence'.

Musgrave Road 'rec' captured on camera around the time the grounds were laid out as a public recreation ground, 1908.

The splendid bowling green at Musgrave Road recreation ground, photographed here in 1926.

The 1st Brookfields Scout group (253rd) was formed in the early 1950s and met at the Methodist church in New Spring Street until 1975. The band was formed around 1955 and finally disbanded after appearing in the Handsworth Scout Gang Show at the Old Rep in Station Street a few years ago. (Alan Smith)

The Brookfields Scouts' coach was stored on land in Clissold Street in the 1960s and early '70s. It was an ex-army coach painted in its original livery of khaki. The two gentlemen photographed here are Group Scout Master Arthur Biddulph and Senior Scout Master Alan Phipps. The photograph was taken before the change in Scout uniform in 1968. (Alan Smith).

Summer camp, around 1975. The original Scout hats were being phased out in favour of the beret at this time. In 1975 the Brookfields Scouts were combined with the All Souls Scout group and moved to new headquarters in Perry Barr. (Alan Smith)

A Sunday school procession from St Cuthbert's church around 1943. The group is in Cuthbert Road. (Janet Ingram)

The splendid façade of the Grove cinema at the bottom of Dudley Road is passed by a tram on the no.55 route in 1938. (David Harvey)

Spring Hill Library provided a library service for a wide area, not just Winson Green and Brookfields but from 1893 for Ladywood as well. Spring Hill library has survived plans to demolish or remove it. However the adjoining shops have not been so fortunate and in fact their replacements, the Brookfields shopping centre, has recently been demolished. At one time Spring Hill was a thriving shopping centre.

eight
Buses and Trams

Above: Roseberry Street bus garage on 21 May 1968. The garage opened originally in 1906 as a Corporation tram depot. After being converted to a bus garage following the closure of the Lodge Road tram route in 1947, it remained in operation until it was shut down in June 1968. It had a capacity of around sixty vehicles. (David Harvey)

Opposite: Two views in Hingeston street. The top photograph shows the BCT tramcar no. 244 outside the Royal Mint public house at the Hingeston Street/Icknield Street junction. The later view is of a no. 96 bus from the late 1960s.

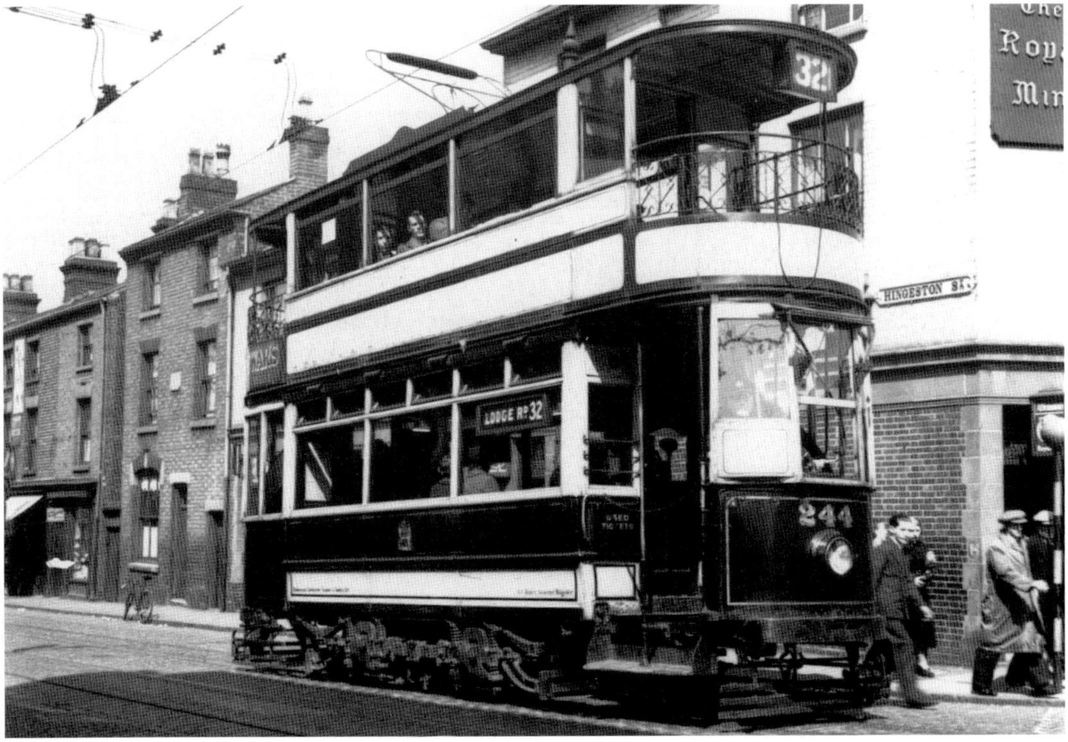
32
LODGE RD 32
244

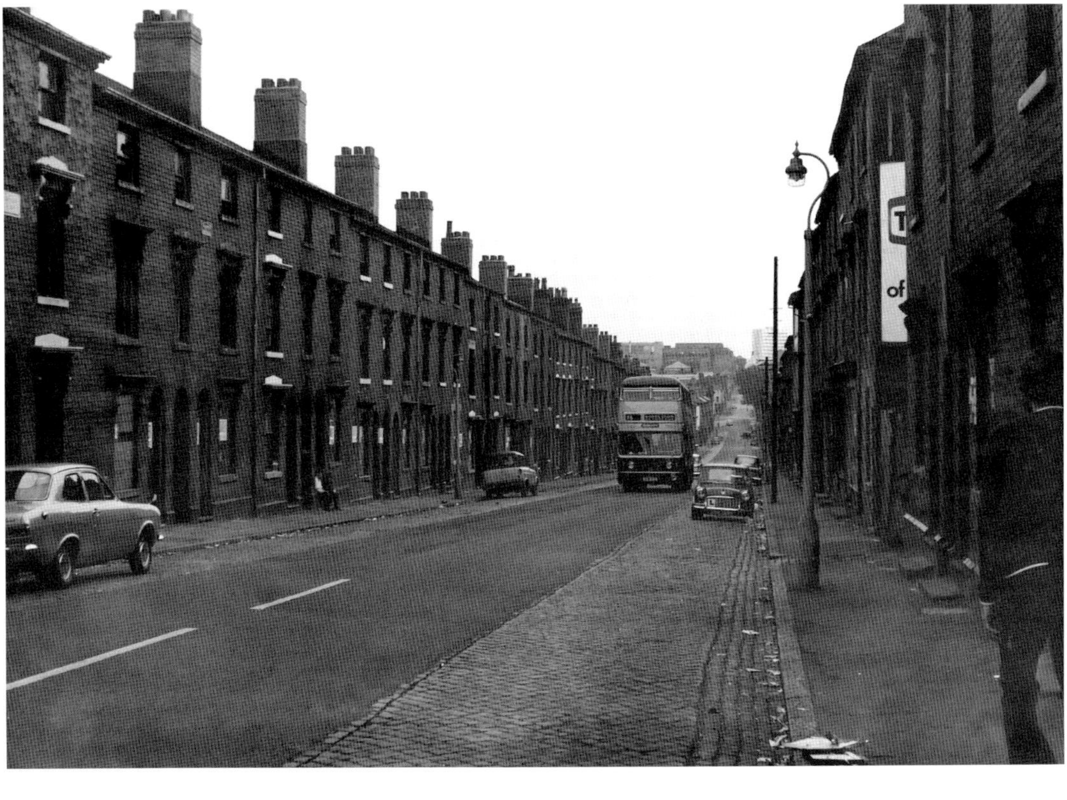

Trams in Lodge Road on the no. 32 route, in the last days of the trams on this route in 1947. 'For the connoisseur perhaps the most fascinating route in the city' as it made its tortuous way from the city centre to Foundry Road. Nicknamed 'The Dipper' it was unique among Birmingham routes in starting it's route under a bridge in Edmund Street in the city centre and finishing under one in Foundry Road. (David Harvey)

On the no. 96 route in Lodge Road in 1969, apparently in a snow storm. (David Harvey)

Two buses working the no. 96 route in around 1962. The top photograph shows a Leyland Atlantean in All Saints Street, the lower one shows a Daimler Fleetline on the Winson Green Road outside Dolman's garage. (David Harvey)

Tramcar no. 843, probably in Ford Street, on a special tour of the city on 23 October 1938. (David Harvey)

The Lodge Road junction with All Saints Street, 28 January 1940. Tramcar no. 262 is fitted with a snow plough to work on the no. 32 route. Buses took over from trams on the Lodge Road route on 30 March 1947, the war interrupting the original plans to change in 1940. (David Harvey)

The Foundry Road terminus, outside the Railway Inn, of the no. 32 tram and the no. 96 bus. The tram is pictured in around 1946, and the Leyland Titan around 1959. (David Harvey).

Left above: Tramcar no. 206 on the no. 31 route in Heath Street, around 1933. (David Harvey)

Left: Again in Heath Street, this time a Daimler CVD6 on the B83 route, around 1965.

Below: Tramcar no. 180 working the no. 29 route on Spring Hill canal bridge on 6 October 1932. The 'B' prefixes indicated joint working with the Birmingham and Midland Motor Omnibus Company (The Midland Red) on routes across Birmingham's boundaries. (David Harvey)

Right: A no. B83 coming into town on Spring Hill, opposite Steward Street, at a time when Spring Hill was a proper shopping centre. The 'B' prefixes were dropped in June 1968. (David Harvey)

Right below: A Leyland Titan working on the B80 route around 1958. It is seen here on the Dudley Road by Summerfield Park, with the school opposite. The Dudley Road bus routes began in October 1939 replacing the trams – the only wartime tramway closures during the war. (David Harvey)

Below: Tramcar no. 102 working on the no. 87 route in Dudley Road, approaching Icknield Port Road on 12 April 1939. The Dudley Road routes were some of the most lucrative for the city. In front of the tramcar is Stanley McKie's pawnshop. The outline of St Patrick's church can be seen in the background. (David Harvey)

Left: Winson Green station was on Winson Green Road not far from Dudley Road. It was on the Stour Valley Line and was built in 1876 for the benefit of the rapidly expanding local population. This view was taken on 11 September 1957, five days before the station finally closed. (Roger Carpenter collection).

Left: Soho and Winson Green station around 1960. The second of the GWR stations north of Snow Hill after Hockley, Soho and Winson Green station opened in 1854. The station closed in 1972 and was disused until the Wolverhamton–Birmingham Metro revived the line and the station as reinvented as Benson Road Metro station. This photograph comes from the Roger Wilson collection of views of GWR stations held in the Social Sciences section of Birmingham Central Library.

A Birmingham tramcar no. 89 at the junction of Heath Street and Dudley Road a few weeks into wartime on 30 September 1939. On one side of the junction is the Lee Bridge Tavern and on the Birmingham side is the furnishing store of Harry Wadley's. Next to the Lee Bridge Tavern were a butcher's, a branch of Freeman Hardy and Willis and a Co-op Branch. (David Harvey).

nine

Street Scenes

Above: The off-licence at No. 265 Camden Street, on the corner with Ellen Street. Corner pubs and small off-licences were an integral part of community life in both Winson Green and Brookfields until redevelopment in the 1960s swept virtually all of them away. (Andrew Maxam)

Opposite: Two views of Don Street in the early years of the last century. The street was a narrow cobbled thoroughfare off Lodge Road with the Don pub on the corner. These photographs show numbers 1-6 and the backs of 39-49.

119

Benson Road about 100 years ago. Jackson's greengrocers was at numbers 35-37.

Sales catalogue for the property on the corner of Winson Green and Dudley Roads. The sale took place on 10 December 1891. A freehold ground rent of £16 1s 5d per annum could be earnt from the three front and four back houses called Clifton terrace.

Two views of numbers 86-96 Devonshire Street. Notice the house numbers chalked on the door in the lower photograph.

Improving the Spring Hill canal bridge in October 1932. The posters at this date were advertising Players cigarettes and Veritas matches as well as attracting customers to the Theatre Royal and the Grove cinema which was showing the long-forgotten film *Amateur Daddy*.

122

Two views from the 1950s. The top photograph is taken looking down Cape Street from Chiswell Street on 22 February 1957, and the lower one shows Wharf Street in November 1958.

Two views from the early 1970s. No. 170 Pitsford Street was the premises for Newman and Field hardware merchants. Typically for this district, this back-street building had had an industrial use from as far back as 1884. At that date Henry McKenzie's electro-plate manufacturers produced their goods there. The lower view is of numbers 20-26 Tudor Street on 27 June 1972, redevelopment looks long overdue for these properties.

Two views from the top of Spring Hill. An atmospheric shot down Spring Hill taken on 3 November 1964 *(above)*. On the left-hand side of the road is Sheffco, tools and files business next to the Guild public house opposite the phone box. On the other side Benjamin Crosby printers can be seen at No. 186 Spring Hill. Regent Motors was next to Clissold Passage by the canal bridge and is photographed here just prior to demolition *(below)* .

Above: Dolman's garage, one of the district's best-known landmarks, opposite the prison on the Handsworth New Road, Lodge Road and Foundry Road junction. The history of the Dolman family's involvement with the business is told in chapter fifteen of Gary Smith's book *A Walk up the Green*. The houses to the right of the garage could well be the oldest houses in the area. They are thought to be outlying houses attached to the original Winson Green House.

Opposite: A study in contrasts. *Above:* The off-licence at numbers 80-82 James Turner Street in July 1951. The licensee was Florence Mary Paice. (Andrew Maxam). *Below:* The new face of the district, desirable properties in Abbey Street, July 1980. Abbey Street commemorates Hockley Abbey, and with this view our photographic journey turns full circle.

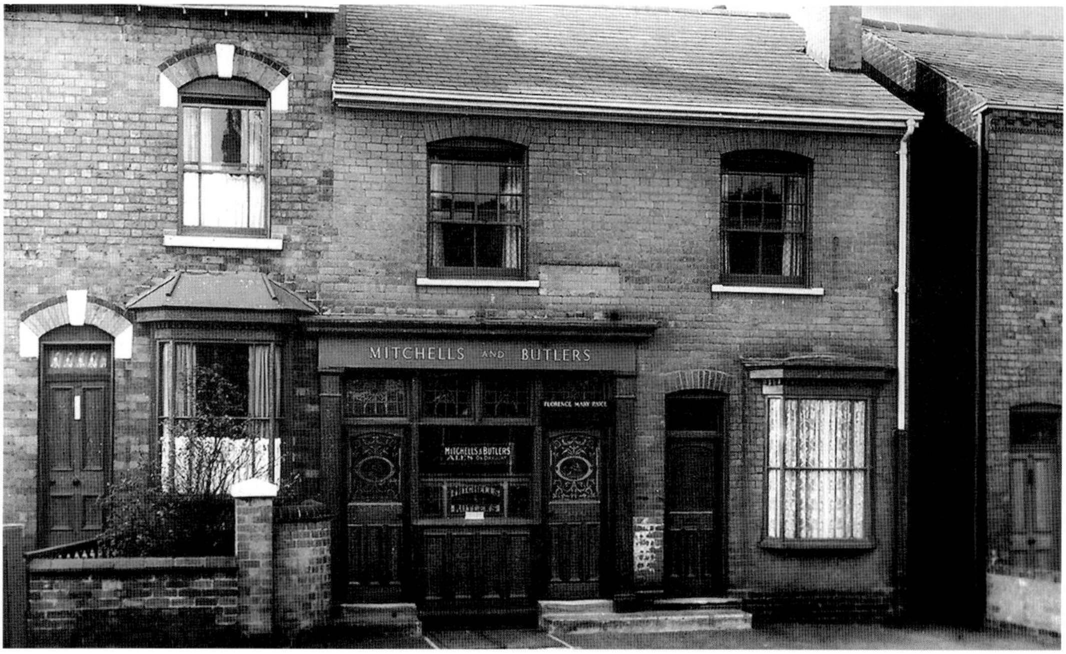
MITCHELLS AND BUTLERS
MITCHELLS & BUTLERS

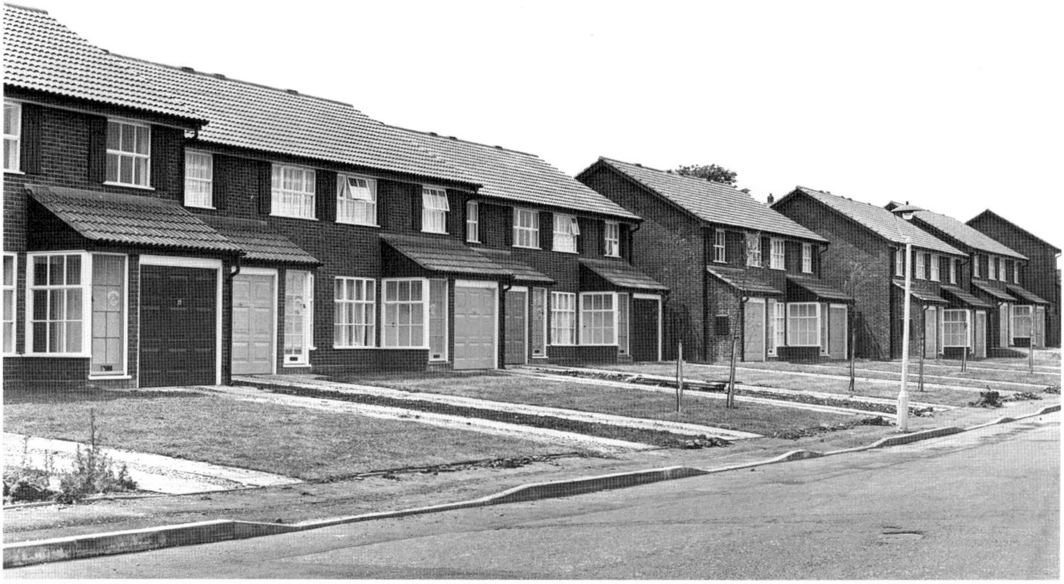

Acknowledgements

The majority of photographs in this book have come from the collections in the Local Studies section of Birmingham Central Library, and I would like to thank all colleagues there for their forbearance while this book was being compiled. All of the un-credited photographs in this book can be viewed in the Central Library and copies made. In particular, thanks goes to Central Library colleagues Andy Willis, Martin Flynn, Joe McKenna, Chris Ash and Margaret Hanson. I am also grateful to Margaret Green, Bernard Gallacher, the staff at E.I.P. Metals Ltd (the old Earle, Bourne & Co.), Ray Shill and Stephen Penker for advice and information.

Various people have lent me photographs which have been used in the book and for whom I hope the book does them justice. Special thanks therefore to Andrew Maxam (pub photographs), David Harvey (trams and buses), Roger Carpenter (railways), Alan Smith (Brookfields Scouts), Francis Whelan (St Patrick's), Linda Chew (Birmingham Co-op), Janet Ingram (St Cuthberts) and Irene Lockwood (Cromwell Hall). David, Roger and Tony Hall have added to the enjoyment of compiling the book by their companionship at the Black Eagle in Factory Road just over the Handsworth border.

This list would not be complete without mentioning the three books written by Gary Smith about his times in Winson Green entitled *A Walk up the Green*, *Winson Green, My World* and *A Trip Down the Flat*. They were invaluable in providing information for the captions. A brilliant website for the area - www.winsongreentobrookfields.co.uk – now exists, from which its driving force Ted Rudge has allowed me to reproduce a number of the photographs. Anyone who is interested in the history of the district or who wishes to relive their time there will really enjoy browsing the site.